THE CROSS TODAY

THE CROSS TODAY

An evaluation of current theological
reflections on the Cross of Christ

Gerald O'Collins, S.J.
Robert Faricy, S.J.
Maurizio Flick, S.J.

PAULIST PRESS
New York/Ramsey/Toronto

Published by Paulist Press

Editorial Office: 1865 Broadway, New York, N.Y. 10023

Business Office: 545 Island Road, Ramsey, N.J. 07446

The following material is used with the permission of the journals indicated, for which the publishers are grateful: 'The Birth of a Theology of the Cross' by Maurizio Flick (*Rassegna di Teologia* July/August 1975), translated by Teresa Martin, R.S.H.M.; 'Teilhard de Chardin's Theology of the Cross' by Robert Faricy (*Horizons* Spring 1976); 'Towards a Theology of the Cross' by Gerald O'Collins (*Rassegna di Teologia* July/August 1977).

ISBN: 0-8091-2116-6

Printed in Hong Kong

232.963

That way the Rosetrees spent their Easter, while for other, less disordered families, Jesus Christ was taken down, and put away, and resurrected, with customary efficiency and varying taste. Outside the churches everyone was smiling to find they had finished with it; they had done their duty, and might continue on their unimpeded way.

Patrick White, *Riders in the Chariot.*

CONTENTS

INTRODUCTION

The theology of the cross has not yet been closely looked at in the English-speaking world or, at least, has not yet been closely looked at by Roman Catholic circles in that world. Maurizio Flick entitled his article contained in this book 'The Birth of a Theology of the Cross'. Beyond the frontiers of France, Germany, Italy and Japan, it might be more accurate to speak of a conception rather than a birth.

How did Catholics (and others) come to their renewed interest in the theology of the cross? And what is the key theme which this theology tackles today?

Maurizio Flick lays his finger on several major reasons for the theology of the cross becoming and remaining a current issue. There are factors in the present cultural situation which fuel interest in 'the word of the cross' (I Cor 1:18). In new ways the old problems of sin, guilt and suffering, especially the suffering of the innocent, clamor for attention. What can the crucifixion say about a world which — so far from ridding itself of sin, suffering and evil — seems more than ever invaded by savagery and torn by fear and greed? Within theology itself the phenomenal growth in biblical studies has enriched our understanding of Christ's passion and death. Furthermore, latterday studies in the history of christian doctrine, particularly those dealing with St Anselm, St Thomas Aquinas and Martin Luther, have provided fresh perspectives which allow us to press beyond some of the old debates and differences about the death of Jesus.

This joint study by three professors at the Gregorian University (Rome) has produced convergent answers to the question: What is the key theme for a theology of the cross? Robert Faricy concludes that 'the dominant meaning of the cross is that it is a passage through death to Jesus Christ'. Maurizio Flick takes the key theme to be suffering accepted within a perspective of faith, so that in Christ such suffering can become an instrument of salvation. My own 'Towards a Theology of the Cross' ends by recalling the pauline theme of 'power made perfect in weakness', which draws its inspiration from the strength of the crucified Christ's utter vulnerability. The responses all pick up the paradox: through death to life (Faricy), salvation in suffering (Flick) and strength in vulnerability (O'Collins).

The three contributors to this book come at the theology of the cross from differing vantage points. Fr Flick's chapter fills in the historical origins of this theology. My own reflections principally concern present directions and progress in thinking about the cross. Fr Faricy views the cross within a universe charged with the dynamic presence of the risen Christ. At times my own contribution tends to treat the cross by itself. Or at least it invites the reader to suspend temporarily belief in the resurrection, so that the full impact of Calvary might be experienced. Fr Flick lists *six* essential features which should be found in any future theology of the cross. Under (1) 'the prolegomena to any discussion of Good Friday', (2) 'the crucifixion itself' and (3) 'our response to that event', I nominate instead *eight* points for any adequate theology of the cross. At the same time, there is considerable overlapping here. Fr Flick's sixth item corresponds to my own last point about the 'existential correlate' to the crucifixion. For that matter his insistence that the cross should be interpreted as part of God's total creative plan (his fifth point) matches the teilhardian approach of Fr Faricy.

Fr Flick and I do not confine ourselves to the work of one thinker but range widely over various contributors to the growing theology of the cross. Fr Faricy devotes his main chapter to that towering presence who continues to loom over Catholic theology, Teilhard de Chardin.

Maurizio Flick has been venerated as a theological professor (and spiritual leader) by generations of American, English, Irish, Scottish and other students at the Gregorian. His publications with Zoltan Alszeghy have contributed to the progress of theology in such areas as original sin and theological anthropology. In 1975 they jointly published what, to my knowledge, is the only full and scientific bibliography on the theology of the cross, *Sussidio bibliografico per una teologia della croce.*

Robert Faricy, the author of *Teilhard de Chardin's Theology of the Christian in the World* (1967) brings a specialist's knowledge to his task. His contribution to this book is enriched through his having been able to use Teilhard's retreat notes (1939-54) and some other unpublished material.

Fr Faricy's 'Teilhard de Chardin's Theology of the Cross' was published in the issue of *Horizons* for Spring, 1976. Fr Flick's article appeared originally in *Rassegna di Teologia* for July/August 1975. For this symposium the footnotes have been slightly abbreviated. I wish to thank Sr Teresa Martin, R.S.H.M. (of Marymount International School, Rome) for her generous kindness in translating Fr Flick's article. My own 'Towards a Theology of the Cross' will be published next month (in Italian) in *Rassegna di Teologia*. These three articles are reprinted by permission. The rest of the material in this book has not been so far published.

We would like to dedicate this book to Father Charles Boyer, the doyen of our theology faculty. We hope that our small symposium expresses and may even further a little our common purpose, a living theology in the service of Jesus Christ, his Church and the world.

Gerald O'Collins, S.J.

The Gregorian University,
June 16, 1977.

1

THE BIRTH OF A THEOLOGY OF THE CROSS

Maurizio Flick, S.J.

It is significant that every now and then in religious and theological literature there is an abundance of publications regarding a particular aspect of the christian mystery. We still recall the explosion of mariological literature in the 1950s; in the 1960s this gave way to an interest in ecclesiology. At the beginning of the 1970s there was a notable movement towards the theology of hope, in its various forms, such as the theologies of earthly realities, of progress, and of liberation.

Ten years ago no one could have foreseen that the moment would come when readers would turn again with ever-increasing interest to that aspect of the christian message, which — after Luther — was called the 'theology of the cross', and seek to appreciate why Christ and the Christian must carry the cross so as to enter into glory.

To observe this phenomenon concretely, we have

published a bibliography containing more than five hundred titles which have mostly appeared within the past decade.[1] Given that the problems treated in these studies have been widely developed in biblical and systematic theology, one can understand the intensity with which the question of 'why the cross?' is posed in contemporary theological literature.

The question is, however, not limited to professional theologians alone; it also involves pastoral workers. In a suggestive and stimulating book, a Roman Catholic curate and a Lutheran minister recently reported how an ecumenical youth group taking an anthropological approach had elaborated in dialogue some answers to this question.[2]

Why is 'The Word of the Cross' a Current Issue?

The first reason is that, in the present cultural situation, the problem of suffering is acutely felt. He who believes in a good Creator is scandalized by suffering, especially by that of the innocent. There are believers who rebel against the figure of the Father who destines his Son for death on a cross.[3] Even those who overcome this scandal feel the need of delving more deeply into the intelligibility of the mystery.[4]

With this instinctive repugnance to pain is connected the crisis about the sense of guilt. In the past, the teaching on original sin (and even more on the 'sins of the world', in which — up to a certain point — even the just are involved) made the necessity of universal suffering more intelligible. At the present time, when the majority of people feel themselves more victims than guilty, the cross, like the sin for which it is the remedy, becomes a problem.[5]

Furthermore, not even the sinner can clearly see how a physical evil can be remedy for a moral evil. At one time the concept was universally accepted of 'vindictive justice' by which punishment restores the order disturbed by sin. Today it has disappeared in lay culture, and in theology is no longer considered an undisputed question.[6] Psychology explains the need for punishment with theories that, apparently, exclude the saving value of the cross. Despite this, many fruitful attempts were made after the last war to utilize intuitions of depth psychology in the theology of the cross.[7] In recent years, it is significant that the works of Moltmann and of Grelot, which differ greatly in their positions, attempt to insert a dialogue between psychology and the doctrine of salvation (soteriology).

Finally, those believers who find conformity with God's will most of all in the work of ending or at least reducing suffering in the world find themselves ill-at-ease before a Christ who, 'in place of the joy which was set before him, took upon himself the cross' (Heb 12:2), and who declared that he who does not take up his cross and follow him is not his disciple (Mt 10:38; Lk 14:27). It is symptomatic that such theologians as Moltmann and Metz feel the necessity of seeking for a theological explanation of the value of the cross which does not contradict either political theology or the theology of hope.[8]

In this whole problem, the influence of Protestant theologians is notable. This can be surprising if we remember the marvelous flowering of theological speculations which Catholic tradition consecrated to the art of reading 'the book of the cross'. And yet, the fundamental experience of today's religious thinker is not so much that of the mystics, who contemplated the harmony of the order of salvation culminating in the cross, but rather the impression of conflict. For this reason Luther felt bound to oppose two theologies, one of glory (which ascends from creatures to the God of the philosophers) and the other of the cross, which comes from amazement before a hidden God who, for inscrutable reasons, exacts suffering.[9] This experience of conflict brought today's Protestant theology, on the one hand, to a courageous confession of faith in the saving value of the cross[10] and, on the other hand, to attempts either (a) to renounce the long-standing concept of a changeless God and to affirm that the Father must suffer in abandoning the Son to death,[11] or (b) to build a 'staurology' (study of the cross), which is no longer preoccupied with man's liberation from sin.[12]

A Re-reading of the Sources

Given the prevalent phenomenological and hermeneutical perspective in contemporary theological research, questions about the cross stimulate above all a re-reading of biblical, patristic and medieval sources, in the light of new problems arising from the cultural environment. Among the 525 titles collected in our bibliography almost half (207) are exegetical monographs, while a quarter (123) study the history of doctrine, and a quarter (116) are dedicated to speculative reflection. The exegetes show a special interest in the synoptic accounts of Christ's passion. The current point of view is indicated by Vatican II: 'The sacred authors, in writing the four Gospels, selected certain of the many elements which had been handed on, either orally or already in written form, others they synthesized or explained with an eye to the situation of the churches, the while sustaining the form of preaching.'[13] Exegetes highlight the characteristic point of view of the individual authors.[14] In the passion, Mark sees the revelation of the Son of God. Matthew recounts it to make the destiny of the Church understood. Luke emphasizes that the suffering Christ precedes his disciples who are called to follow him.[15] The exegetes are also interested in how the accounts were developed, and what their relation was to the original facts.[16] Research into the 'historical Jesus', who is conceptually distinguishable from the 'Christ of faith', tends to understand better the didactic intention peculiar to each individual author. It determines to what extent certain schemes adopted by them can be replaced by others more understandable today. It wants to ensure the facts which today's Church must proclaim in today's thought forms and apply them to the emerging questions of present-day existence. Granted, however, that not only the results, but also the very methods of research are pretty much questioned in exegetical literature,[17] the sober criticism, expressed above all by English-language exegetes,[18] seem to be well founded. In particular it seems unacceptable to consider as a unique norm of orthodoxy and orthopraxis what, according to some particular scholar, the historical Jesus would have done and said. The inspired interpretation of the sacred writers is always the norm for us. While they may not record the historical event with mechanical exactitude, they do express the meaning faithfully. We fear that in this regard there exists a certain tension between the prevalent tendencies in exegesis and dogma.[19]

The decisive importance of this problem appears in the use that the theologian makes of the johannine doctrine of the passion. Characteristic of this is the interpretation of the death on the cross as an 'exaltation' of the Lord,[20] who has fully 'completed' his whole mission. We will probably never be able to determine exactly which words Christ pronounced on the cross. But if we hold that the entire historic reality of the cross is expressed in the cry: 'My God, why have you abandoned me?' (Mk 15:34; Mt 27:44), while the sentences, 'Father into your hands I commend my spirit' (Lk 23:44) and 'All is fulfilled' (Jn 19:30), are legendary accretions not corresponding to the historic reality, we fail to see what value the johannine soteriology still has. If instead we accept all three sentences as perhaps not uttered historically but as true interpretations of historical reality (Jesus, although feeling himself abandoned, gave himself faithfully and courageously to the Father and with that fulfilled his mission), we find the basis for a full participation in the Church's doxology: 'We adore you, O Christ, and we bless you because by your holy cross you have redeemed the world.'[21] It seems to us that one of the characteristics that distinguishes the Catholic theologies of the cross is this Catholic way of understanding the abandonment of Christ on the cross. It permits us to interpret the cross within a synthesis dominated by the idea of a God who creates and governs the world to make it participate in his goodness.

As regards Paul's 'word of the cross', besides the synthetic monographs,[22] there are many studies on individual themes of pauline soteriology, for example on the servant of Jahweh,[23] redemption, and sacrifice.[24]

The *history of christian doctrine* is obviously not overlooked in current research on the foundations for a theology of the cross. The history of the symbolism and the cult of the cross has been developed in detail, a fact which has made the link between theology and church life more intelligible.[25] Numerous monographs analyze the way in which individual theologians of the patristic and medieval eras interpreted the efficacy of the Lord's passion and death.[26] In particular the theories of St Anselm, St Thomas and Luther have been studied intensively. The results of these studies are surprising in two ways.

Above all, it has become clear how difficult it is to divide the representatives of christian thought into rigid classes, schools or currents. Polemical Catholic theology was, for a long time, used to the categories proposed by Jean Rivière:[27] one could distinguish the mythical, physico-mystical, moral, juridical tendencies, with their many sub-divisions. Protestant theologians generally found their bearings according to the triple classification of the Swedish scholar, Gustaf Aulén.[28] But, if we wish to insert any one author into a definite category, the system shows itself to be unusable. An example of this is the discussion among historians about assigning a place to Luther. It began by affirming a fundamental opposition between the Reformer and the scholastics,[29] but presently there is a tendency to admit just a change of accent.[30] One has the impression that the differences between authors apply rather to the conceptual apparatus they use for interpretation than to the fundamental intuition that they wish to express.[31]

The second result of historical research is this. While we accept the basic intention of each father and doctor of the Church as witnessing to the perennial faith in the soteriological value of the cross, we have reservations on the value of their contingent categories. In other ages these categories facilitated an understanding of the mystery; today they cause difficulties.[32]

Finally, we must recognize that so far research has overlooked the relations between the cross of Jesus and that of the Christian. Certainly there exists abundant literature on suffering in general and on its particular aspect (death, illness, and various setbacks). But in all this the 'theology of the cross' is not yet the organizing principle. For this reason we must single out the monographs (in our bibliography we have indicated a hundred of them) which emphasize this aspect, whether this aspect be in scripture[33] or in the history of christian doctrine.[34]

The Basic Orientations for a 'Treatise'

Exegesis, history and the church's magisterium offer very varied material on the meaning of the cross. A Catholic preacher has said both in word and in a book

7

(which was widely circulated and discussed) that Jesus died in vain.[35] The Council of Trent, however, presupposes as the basis of all doctrinal development on the Mass that Christ, 'our God and Lord, wished to offer himself to the Father on the altar of the cross, so as, through his death, to fulfil the redemption'.[36] The range of such contradictions is so extensive and profound that it seems impossible at present to formulate a series of assertions capable of obtaining the agreement of all the exegetes, historians, and theologians.

In the face of this chaos, the situation of theology is similar to the conditions in which, according to St Thomas[37] and St Bonaventure[38], theologians of their time found themselves, when confronted with the material from which our classical treatises were then built. We deal with a 'dark forest' of affirmations, in which neither a track ahead nor a conclusive meaning can be found. At present reflection on the cross is entering into that phase of doctrinal development which produces 'Summas'. The paradoxical affirmations of past documents (the *sic et non*) have fulfilled their aim. We have come to realize that many stereotyped models for preaching are no more than contingent forms of the message of salvation. Now we need to formulate in our own language what the word on the cross says to us. Such a formulation, naturally, will not be effected in one bound, but in the measure in which we can progressively hammer out the fundamental conceptual clarifications.[39] We limit ourselves here to proposing a few vital points for the doctrinal whole which is being formed.

(1) The death of Jesus on the cross is an event that is essential for our salvation, not only insofar as we know it, but also objectively, in itself. This conviction so penetrated the faith of the Church right from the first revelations transmitted to us, that if it should prove mistaken, the truth of christian faith would be compromised.

(2)   The intelligibility of this mystery of salvation must be sought within the horizon of faith in God, the lover of life.   The notion of a Father who wants physical evil for its own sake is not only opposed to human intelligence, but is not documented in revelation.

(3)   The Father delights in the event of the cross, and Christ accepts the painful death (although feeling a repugnance of the flesh), because the cross is an essential conditioning and the connatural expression of the most perfect human self-realization: against the rupture of sin, Christ, hoping against hope, and abandoning himself into his Father's hands, fulfilled that perfection for which God created the world.

(4)   The efficacy of the event of the cross for the salvation of humanity can be explained not so much in an ascending plan (Christ appeases the angry Father), but rather in a descending plan (Christ is the instrument chosen by the Father to renew humanity). However, to explain this effectiveness, it would seem more appropriate to speak of Christ the 'sacrament of salvation', rather than *only* of Christ's merits and satisfaction.

(5)   In this way, the cross no longer seems an unforeseen contingent event which heals a breakdown in the plan of God, but it becomes part of the creative plan. The Father loves the Son, who is made flesh to become, during all his life, but especially through the cross, a 'glorious conqueror'.   He wishes all humanity to participate in the glorious image of the crucified Son, so that he will be the first born of many brothers (cf. Rom 8:29).   Thus in germ the glory of the resurrection is present on the cross, and the resurrection, the climax of creation, is only the complete development of the glory initiated on the cross.

(6)   Men are called to follow Christ: for them, too, their cross is an existential conditioning and the connatural expression of their own maturity, both human and christian. They truly become disciples when (challenged by their own cross) they fulfil, and (carrying

the cross) they express, their own fundamental option for God, and that in a world signed by sin. It is very important to emphasize that the cross is carried not only by the patient endurance of evil, but also by fighting against the evils which oppress humanity. 'The flesh and the world' do not hesitate to put the cross on the shoulders of those who seek peace and justice.[40]

Thus each disciple of Jesus Christ, carrying (passively and actively) his own cross, witnesses to salvation and makes others participate in salvation. He too becomes for others a mediator and co-redeemer, under the sole mediator and co-redeemer, Jesus Christ.

In order that a treatise on the theology of the cross may be adequately developed, one must not limit oneself to gathering a list of assertions, isolated from the rest of the message, but one must penetrate in some way into the whole understanding of the christian mystery. In fact, a treatise is fully developed only when it means that, with an 'about-face', all theology may be considered from the point of view it expresses. (This has recently occurred, for example, with anthropology and with pneumatology). In this way, the 'theology of the cross' will examine the cross of each man, the cross that has meaning even for the innocent, the cross of the fallen man, the cross of the Christian, and the cross of the Church, consistently using the cross of Christ as its interpretative key.

Naturally the theology of the cross must not be confused with the problem of evil (which includes physical as well as moral evil, and treats equally the suffering of the just man and the sinner). The theology of the cross has as its direct object that suffering freely accepted within the perspective of faith. And even if this theology does not explain the reason for all suffering, it shows how any kind of suffering can be transformed into an instrument of salvation, insofar as the Christian either fights against it, or accepts it to live and die with Jesus Christ.

As can be seen from this presentation, no treatise on the theology of the cross has yet been totally formed. But we do have a quarry from which one can seek to build a new expression of the message of faith.

2

TEILHARD DE CHARDIN'S THEOLOGY
OF THE CROSS

Robert Faricy, S.J.

The religious thought of Pierre Teilhard de Chardin, the Jesuit priest-scientist whose principal life-work was to try to reformulate christian truths in terms of contemporary thought categories, was little known at the time of his death twenty years ago.[1] In the 1960s he was fashionable, his name a household word for Catholic intellectuals and a banner for the more aggressive promoters of Catholic renewal. Today, the Teilhard fad has passed, and serious scholarship is re-evaluating his contribution to christian theology. Almost all his books and essays have been published (the final volume will appear soon), over thirty doctoral dissertations on his religious ideas have been written in the past five years, and his letters and diaries are gradually appearing in published form. One fact that is becoming increasingly clear is that the cross occupies a key position in Teilhard's writings.

Teilhard's thought has a three-tiered structure. At a first level is his theory of evolution.[2] He sees evolution continuing after the appearance of man, taking place now in society in the form of human progress. The focus of this theory of evolution is man-in-society. At a second level, Teilhard interprets some of the traditional christological data in the framework of his theory of evolution; this results in a christology which has as its center the risen Christ especially in the mystery of his second coming. It is, then, an eschatological christology that centers not so much on Jesus crucified as on Jesus risen who is the future focal point of all true progress. At the third level of his thought, Teilhard builds a spiritual theology, a spirituality, based on his christology. This spirituality is the content of his greatest work, *The Divine Milieu*.[3] It is a spiritual theology of the cross. It is true, of course, that the central axis of Teilhard's entire spiritual doctrine is the interpersonal relationship between the Christian and the risen Jesus; but this relationship is lived out by the Christian in and through the world. Just as Teilhard's christology is a theology of Jesus as he is now, risen, so his spirituality is a theology of the christian life as it is to be lived now, in this world. And, although Jesus is risen, the Christian who is following him in this world is, as Jesus was, in the existential structure of the cross. So, like any truly christian spirituality, Teilhard's is a spirituality of the cross. Furthermore, because Teilhard's whole system of thought, beginning with his theory of evolution and including his christology, is ordered to his spirituality, and because his spirituality is dominated by the cross, it is—from this point of view—the cross that is central to his thought.

In this chapter, I will first briefly describe the place of the cross in Teilhard's christology. There will follow an outline of Teilhard's spiritual doctrine of the cross in christian life. Finally, I will consider the role of the cross in Teilhard's understanding of death.

Robert Faricy

The Cross of Jesus

The christian answer to the classic problem of evil is the redemption. Why, if God is good and loving, do death and hatred and violence exist? Why is there so much suffering, failure, pain, misunderstanding? Why is sinfulness part of the human condition? Christianity has always responded to these questions by saying that Jesus saves men from sin and death and, finally, from every evil; that there will be a time when 'there will be no more death, and no more mourning or sadness, for the world of the past will be finished';[4] and that man's suffering and death in this world are, or can be, somehow, a share in the suffering and death of Jesus.

The doctrine of the redemption has been formulated theologically in various ways according to diverse cultures. That is, at different times in the history of christian thought, different models—conditioned by the cultures they existed in—were used to express and to explain the mystery of the redemption.

In early Christianity, the eastern fathers of the Church, Justin, Irenaeus, Origen, and later Athanasius, Basil, Gregory of Nyssa, and Gregory of Nazianzus, used the widely spread and well known institution of slavery as a cultural model. Man was a slave to sin and death. Jesus, through his death on the cross paid the necessary ransom to free man from slavery to the power of darkness. In the early Middle Ages, the cultural model of Roman law was dominant in the theology of the redemption. Man has transgressed against God; the penalty for the crime must be proportionate both to the offense and to the dignity of the person offended. Only an infinite person can make satisfaction for man's sins. Much modern English Protestant theology has used the idea of Augustine, and later of Abelard, of 'moral influence': Jesus' passion and death move man to turn to God in conversion of heart.

14

Teilhard, too, uses a culturally conditioned model to present the mystery of Jesus' redemptive death. As early as 1929 Teilhard could see that Catholic theology of redemption, under the pressure of an emerging evolutionary world-view, was beginning to change;[5] he writes:

> To the informed eye, is there not already a barely perceptible change of shade? Original sin is very gradually becoming, is it not, something more in the nature of a tough beginning than a fall? The Redemption more akin to a liberation than a sacrifice? The cross more evocative of hard-won progress than of penitential expiation?[6]

Teilhard's aim in using an evolutionary model to express the mystery of the cross is in no way to minimize the place of the cross in theology, but rather in order to underline 'the truth, the power, and the irresistible appeal of the cross'.[7]

In Teilhard's theological vision, Jesus risen is the future focal point of the world's forward movement; the risen Christ is the goal of history and of all true progress. The world, then, is understood as in evolution, as in-the-making. The process of evolution, having produced man, is now — in man — conscious of itself; and it takes the form of human progress. Teilhard transposes the relationship between the world and Christ risen, as it is found in the letters of Saint Paul, so that the relationship can be understood in terms of a future-oriented and evolutionary world-view that sees history, genesis, and development as essential dimensions of reality. It is a perspective in which the world is understood as holding together in Christ, as a world existing in Christ and depending on him for its very existence. It is not a static world, but a dynamic one, and it is moving toward a divinely fixed and proclaimed goal: the ultimate reconciliation of all things in Christ. This is Teilhard's 'cosmic Christ', although it is not so much Christ who is cosmic as it is the world that is christic. It is a faith vision of reality that sees everything dependent on the risen Lord for its very being, and that sees his influence in everything. To a great extent, this is the vision of Vatican II's Pastoral Constitution on the Church in the Modern World, *Gaudium et spes,* which depends in many ways on Teilhard's christology, especially in the introduction and the first section.

The risen Jesus, then, is the active focus of the world's convergence; and, further, he is the divine influence that pulls the world forward into the future and towards the final recapitulation of all things in himself. This helps to explain the importance of the Eucharist in Teilhard's christology. For the same Christ in whom the world holds together and toward whom it is moving is present in the Eucharist. In his real presence, Jesus makes present, in himself, and in an anticipatory way, the ultimate future of the world, and of each person — for he contains that ultimate future in himself. This is the basis for Teilhard's christian optimism: that Jesus, who holds every man's future and the whole world's future in his hands, is present now in the world, in the Church, and in a special way in the Eucharist. Teilhard's optimism is not a blind faith in progress; he was well aware of the ambiguities of progress and the misuses of freedom. It is, rather, a hope in Jesus who has risen and gone ahead, but who is present.

But what is the place of the cross of Jesus in this understanding of the relationship between Christ and the world? In order to become the central element of the world, Christ had, first of all, to *be* an element of the world; and this, for Teilhard, is the fundamental reason for the incarnation. Teilhard writes that

for Christ to make his way into the world by

any side-road would be incomprehensible.
. . . The smallness of Christ in the cradle, and
the even tinier forms that preceded his appearance among men, are more than a moral lesson
in humility. They are in the first place the
application of a law of birth and, following on
from that, the sign of Christ's definitively taking
possession of the world. It is because Christ
was 'inoculated' in matter that he can no longer
be dissociated from the growth of the Spirit:
that he is so engrained in the visible world that
he could henceforth be torn away from it only
by rocking the foundations of the universe.[8]

In Teilhard's theology of Christ's redemptive death,
the cross of Jesus has two aspects. The negative aspect
of Christ's redemptive work of the cross is reparation
for evil, compensation for sinful disorder in the world.
It is, however, the positive aspect of Christ's death on
the cross that Teilhard stresses: the effort of reconciliation. By his death, Jesus reconciled, in principle and
in a way that is being worked out in history, all things
in himself; he reconciled the world with God, and the
various elements of the world among themselves. It is
this side of the redemptive act of the cross that is upper-
most in Teilhard's thought: that Jesus, by his death,
unified the world with God and within itself. The cross
of Jesus is seen, then, above all as a work of unification.

Christ, it is true, is still he who bears the sins
of the world; moral evil is in some mysterious
way paid for by suffering. But, even more
essentially, Christ is he who structurally in
himself, and for all of us, overcomes the resistance to unification offered by the multiple,
the resistance to the rise of spirit inherent in
matter. Christ is he who bears the burden,
constructionally inevitable, of every creation.
He is the symbol and the sign-in-action of pro-

gress.   The complete and definitive meaning of redemption is no longer *only to expiate*: it is to surmount and conquer.[9]

In Teilhard's earliest written reference to the theology of the cross, in 1915, in his private wartime journal, he wrote: 'evolution: *the suffering Christ* reveals to us its hard work and what it is like, and he helps us to carry the weight.   And so the *cross* is brought into human becoming'.[10]   A little later, in the same diary, he writes: 'The cross is the symbol of work more than of penance (the penance being in the work).'[11]   This embryonic concept, scribbled in a notebook at the front during the First World War, takes fuller form thirty years later in the essays written just after the Second World War.   'The suffering Christ, without ceasing to be "he who bears the sins of the world," indeed precisely as such...(is) "he who bears and supports the weight of the world in evolution".'[12]   Jesus, 'with the sins, bears the whole weight of the world in progress.'[13]

Why is it, if the cross has such an important place in Teilhard's christology, that he seems to attach so little importance to personal sin?   It is true that Teilhard has a spiritual theology of the cross that is based on his theology of redemption, but where in all this is personal sin?   It seems to be missing, at least for the most part. This is not because Teilhard was unaware of the importance of sin, nor because it did not, somehow, 'fit into his system.'   Rather Teilhard, in not underlining the importance of personal sin, was reacting to what he considered to be an overemphasis on it in the Catholic tradition since the Middle Ages.   His idea of sin is a realistic, quite unromantic, view: sin is simply evil at the level of human freedom.   He did not stress sin because, as he writes in a letter to Father Gaston Fessard, 'I can hardly fail to see that the enormous penitential theory of Catholicism is an *hypertrophie* of the notion of evil—

or even a slightly morbid distortion inclining the faithful to see only the dark and negative face of things.'[14]

The Cross and Christian Life

The cross of Jesus, the historical act of his suffering and death, was the reconciliation of all things in himself, the redemptive effort of uniting all things in himself. Therefore, the cross is the symbol not only of reparation for sin but, profoundly, of progress made in hard labor and suffering. Teilhard makes this clear in a letter late in his life: 'Decidedly, and making a play on words, one might say that at this time what is "crucial" is the meaning of the cross: mere expiation? or, more broadly, expression-symbol of the "evolutive effort" of spiritualization, with its two aspects of conquest and of suffering? I am convinced that it is only this "second cross" that is capable of (and destined to be) the world's salvation.'[15] 'The Cross', Teilhard writes in his World War I journal, 'preaches and symbolizes the hard work of renunciation..., the cross is both the condition and the way of progress.'[16]

About the same time, in an early essay, Teilhard writes that 'the road our Savior followed' is the way of the cross that man is 'called on to follow with him.'[17] Furthermore, because of the very nature of reality, the 'truth about our position in this world is that in it we are on a cross'; it is in Jesus crucified that 'every man can recognize his own true image'.[18] What is the meaning of the cross in the life of the Christian? Teilhard has two approaches to an answer to the question. At one level, he discusses the symbolism of the cross for today's Christian, what the cross as a symbol stands for. At another and more practical level, he describes the asceticism of the cross in daily life, and its place in progress towards greater union with God.

For Teilhard, the cross is the symbol of all real

progress. It is 'the symbol not merely of the dark retrogressive side of the universe in genesis, but also and, even more, of its triumphant and luminous side'.[19] It is 'the symbol of progress and victory won through mistakes, disappointments, and hard work'.[20] Although over half the entire central section of the spiritual classic *The Divine Milieu* is devoted to the spiritual theology of the cross in christian life, there are a few pages where Teilhard writes precisely of the cross's symbolism. For example:

> The royal road of the cross is no more nor less than the road of human endeavor supernatur- ally righted and prolonged. Once we have fully grasped the meaning of the cross, we are no longer in danger of finding life sad and ugly. We shall simply have become more at- tentive to its barely comprehensible solemnity.[21]

It might be thought that this view reduces the mystery of the cross, or at least its symbolism, to a simply natural plane, but this would be an error. Here perhaps more than anywhere else in Teilhard's writings one finds the natural and the supernatural orders understood as completely distinct but as fully integrated. The cross stands not merely for human reality but, beyond that, for the assumption and integration by God in Jesus of all that is human. When Teilhard speaks of the cross, even as a symbol, he means the christian cross; that is, Jesus crucified.[22] And he never reduces the mystery to mere symbolism, as though reality and symbol were separable. He concludes the section in *The Divine Milieu* on the meaning of the cross with these words:

> To sum up, Jesus on the cross is both the symbol and the reality of the immense labor of the centuries which has, little by little, raised up the created spirit and brought it back to the depths of the divine milieu. He represents

(and in a true sense, he is) creation, as, up-
held by God, it reascends the slope of being,
sometimes tearing itself from things in order to
pass beyond them, and always compensating,
by physical suffering, for the setbacks caused
by moral downfalls. ...The Christian is not
asked to swoon in the shadow, but to climb
in the light, of the cross.[23]

For an understanding of Teilhard's theology of the
cross, the most important of his essays is 'What the
World is Looking for from the Church of God at This
Moment: A Generalizing and Deepening of the Meaning
of the Cross.'[24] This short essay is in the form of a
plea to the Church to make clearer the meaning of the
cross, to present the cross in such a way that it can be
seen as the answer to man's aspirations. 'Christianity'
Teilhard writes, 'is pledged to the cross and dominated
by the sign of the cross, by its birth and for all time.
It cannot remain itself except by identifying itself ever
more intensely with the essence of the cross.'[25] But
what is the essence of the cross, its true meaning? In
a letter to a friend a few years earlier, Teilhard had
written that 'the idea of a value of sacrifice and pain for
the sake of sacrifice and pain itself (whereas the value
of pain is simply to pay for some useful conquest!) is
a dangerous (and very "Protestant") perversion of the
"meaning of the cross" (the true meaning of the cross
is: "Toward progress through effort").'[26]

In his essay on the meaning of the cross, Teilhard
goes on to point out that, even for Catholics, the cross
has been primarily a symbol of atonement and of expiation. It has carried a whole complex of connotations
and meanings; among them may be distinguished three
unfortunate tendencies: a vision of the world as dominated by evil and death, an attitude of mistrust toward
man, and a mistrust of the material. All this, of course,
is secondary to the love of God for man, and to the

love man is called to have for the crucified Lord, both of which are, more basically, what the cross stands for. But the question is precisely here: how can that love be shown not only without the quasi-Manichean connotations but in a more true and, therefore, more appealing way? By restoring to the symbolism of the cross two elements which belong to it properly: the transcendent and the ultra-human (the supernatural) that man is called to. This can be done, Teilhard goes on, by understanding the cross as synthesizing these two: the transcendent, the 'above', the 'upward' impulse of man toward the worship of God; and the ultra-human, the 'up ahead', the 'forward' impulse of man towards building a better future. For this is what Jesus has done by his cross, and what man does by participating in the cross of Jesus: to raise up the world, to move it upward and forward, closer to God and closer to its own final point of maturation. The cross, then, must finally be seen and presented in terms of what it truly is: the act and the symbol of all real progress.

In the notes of his annual retreat in 1941, Teilhard writes that the cross should be understood in such a way that 'we can present it to the world with enthusiasm. It should (must) shock the loafers and egoists; it *should not* be a scandal for those at the forefront of human progress.'[27] Earlier in the same notes, after praying over the traditional christian idea of suffering in union with Christ suffering, Teilhard writes: 'What a strange idea of the mystics and of piety: to suffer *because* Our Lord is suffering! But Our Lord is associated with suffering (is in suffering) precisely because he is the LOCUS and the beginning of total change (*renversement*).' He adds that true compassion is a participating in the *action* of the cross.[28] In a later retreat, he distinguishes two classic ways of making the 'Stations of the Cross': 'in compassion with Christ; and in compassion with all human suffering at the time (grief, anguish).'[29]

On the Good Friday just before his death at Easter 1955, Teilhard wrote to his friend and provincial superior, Father Ravier, regarding the meaning of the cross.

> The meaning of the cross—I have nothing substantial to add to the few pages I sent you in September 1952: 'What the World is Looking for from the Church of God at This Moment: A Generalizing and Deepening of the Meaning of the Cross'.
>
> What I thought when I wrote that (and when I wrote *The Divine Milieu*) I am more convinced of now than ever. In a universe in progressive development, . . . the cross (without losing its expiatory or compensating function) becomes the symbol and the expression of 'evolution' in its fullest sense. . . . .
>
> And so, without attenuating the christian tradition, it becomes possible to present to today's world the cross, not only as a 'consolation' for the world's miseries but as a 'stimulant' (the most complete and the most dynamic stimulant that exists) to make progress and to go as far as possible, on earth, for God. . . . .

Teilhard continues the letter complaining that at present even the most brilliant and penetrating contemporary Jesuit thinkers are still reflecting in a static rather than in a dynamic and evolutionary framework. He concludes:

> But tomorrow . . . the crucified God (qua-crucified) will have become the spiritual mover the most powerful possible (because the most valorizing and the only 'amorizing') of ultra-humanization. That is my faith, that I would like to proclaim publicly before I die.[30]

Teilhard's ascetical theology is the translation into practical terms of what the cross symbolizes. This teaching is found in its fullest form in *The Divine Milieu*. Summarized very briefly, it consists in three phases, or modes.

First of all, *centration*.[31] Man's first duty is to build and to find himself, to become himself, to grow as a person. 'First, develop yourself, Christianity says to the Christian.'[32]. This is, of course, a life-time program: to develop personally, to unify one's ideas and feelings and behavior, to grow in christian maturity.

Secondly, *decentration*. This means that one cannot reach the limits of his personal development, nor even arrive at anything like maturity of person, without going out of oneself and uniting with others. 'If you possess something, Christ says in the Gospel, leave it and follow me.'[33] 'Decentration' is Teilhard's one-word condensation of the Gospel injunction to renunciation, to lose oneself for the sake of the kingdom so as to find oneself, just as the seed must fall into the ground in order to bear fruit. There exists in each man the elementary temptation that, in order to grow as a person, it is necessary to be egotistical, to be selfish, to work primarily for one's own fulfillment; it is the illusion that to be more means to possess more. But, Teilhard points out, we grow only by emerging from ourselves to unite with others. *Centration* and *decentration* are not chronological steps but two phases of one dialectical process. They go together necessarily, and they lead into the third phase of Teilhard's dialectic movement of christian perfection, *surcentration,* the subordination of man's life to a life greater than his own. This is the phase of union with God, of being centered not on oneself but on Christ. So, through *decentration,* through renunciation, man becomes less centered on himself and more centered on Christ as he shares in Christ's cross.

Centration, decentration, surcentration, are, of

course, the categories of the paschal mystery: life, death, resurrection. Just as the life of Jesus was a building toward the final decentration which was his death on the cross and was a passage to his risen life, so too the Christian's life is a continuous building and a fragmenting and a coming apart in order to come together again less centered on self and more centered on Jesus Christ. Christian life as a process toward holiness is, in its dialectical movement, a participation in the life, in the cross, and in the resurrection of Jesus.

Far from being an asceticism of flight from the world, Teilhard's spirituality of the cross is a program of involvement in the world, a *kenosis* that is a way of the cross that leads to resurrection. In this perspective, even the most cloistered contemplative life can be seen as a profound involvement in the world because it is a radical kenosis, a plunge into the heart of the world in order to be as completely as possible centered on Christ who is the Heart of the world.

For Teilhard, then, there is no conflict between cross and involvement in the world; the two go together by nature of the very structure of reality. During Teilhard's lifetime, as well as after, this approach was neither understood nor appreciated by some of the best known thinkers in the Church. Teilhard's correspondence with Maurice Blondel in December 1919, shows anything but a meeting of minds on the relationship between attachment to human progress and christian renunciation.[34] Less well known is Teilhard's public exchange with Gabriel Marcel in 1947. The great difference between the view of Teilhard and the Catholic existentialism of Marcel is clear from the following excerpt from the notes of the debate.

> *P. T. de Chardin:* Man, in order to be man, must have humanly tried everything, to the end . . .

G. Marcel: That is an anti-christian idea, and leads to Promethean man.

P. T. de Chardin: Man, if he reflects on what he is doing, finds himself led to perceive that he must go out of himself in order to attain the summit. What makes man Promethean is the refusal to go beyond his own action. Prometheus is trapped into a total death.

G. Marcel: The more man works in the direction that you indicate, the more he puts himself under conditions that make humility difficult.

P. T. de Chardin: We feel ourselves to depend on God all the more as we realize our weakness.

G. Marcel: If there is progress, then self-mastery has nothing to do with progress.

P. T. de Chardin: Self-mastery and the mastery of the world go together.[35]

This dialogue, although perhaps not easy to follow, needs no comment. It points up the originality of Teilhard's thinking as well as showing how far removed he was from the pessimism of post-World War II European existentialism.

The Cross and Death

The emphasis in this chapter so far has been, as it is in Teilhard's books and essays and in his letters, on the positive aspect of the cross. Even though, and particularly in *The Divine Milieu,* that dimension of the cross which implies renunciation, diminishment, failure, and death is often brought out eloquently and at length, in general Teilhard presents the positive aspect of the cross, the cross as the symbol and the reality of progress through suffering and hard labour. This is not usually the case in his private notes and particularly in his retreat notes.

In his own spiritual life, more and more as he grew older, Teilhard paid special attention to the negative side of the cross, and especially to the cross as the symbol of christian death. In his earlier essays and private notes, he considers death with a certain scientific objectivity: in an evolutionary world, death is a law, 'the regular indispensable condition of the replacement of one individual by another'.[36] At the same time, death is man's worst weakness and worst enemy, the sum of all the evils of the universe; it is 'the epitome, and the common basis, of everything that terrifies us',[37] and 'the form *par excellence* of the inevitable, menacing, newness-bringing Future'.[38]

Jesus, however, has transformed death by his own death on the cross. 'In itself death is a failure and a stumbling-block.'[39] But Christ has 'vanquished death. He gave it, physically, the value of a metamorphosis: through which the world, with him, entered into God.'[40] Christian death, then, is the final decentration.[41]

It is principally in the personal notes of his retreats that one finds Teilhard underlining the negative aspect of the cross by which it stands for christian death as a participation in the death of Christ. He made the Spiritual Exercises of Saint Ignatius Loyola for eight days every year; ordinarily, when making the Spiritual Exercises, one prays about death in the first of the four sections or phases of the Exercises, the section treating of sorrow for sin. Teilhard, however, frequently—and always after his 1941 retreat—meditated on death in the third phase of the Exercises, on the passion and death of Jesus. The meaning of the cross for him personally in his retreat notes is, above all, that it represents, and is, his own ageing and his forthcoming death, both as a share in the cross of Christ. This is the same spiritual theology of the cross that is found in Teilhard's published writings; it is the same cross that is the symbol of progress as well as the symbol of death. But it is this

27

negative dimension rather than the positive that one finds Teilhard himself praying over in his retreats.[42]

Death for Teilhard opens out to 'the Unknown'.[43] He asks himself in his retreat journal: 'How is it that death does not kill, and in what measure truly does it kill, the taste for life? In fact, we live forgetting about death, and when death approaches, we lose the taste for life, or at least we risk losing it.'[44] He writes of the irreconcilability of death and action,[45] and of the double duty of docility to death and of a renewal of youthful spirits.[46]

Sometimes, the problem of his own anxiety in the face of death preoccupies Teilhard. In his sixtieth year, in the notes on his retreat, he records two anxiety provoking questions regarding death: 'Will Jesus be there? Will he take me or reject me? I can fear the second possibility; yet, it should challenge and encourage me.'[47] A few years later, during another retreat, he writes that, 'in the last analysis, the only true suffering and trial is *doubt*; nothing would be hard *if* one were sure that there is a Jesus on the other side.'[48] And a year after that: 'As if Christ were *not* real for me. Should it be normal that Christ leave untouched the sensible surface of anguish and that he work more deeply, never at the level of what is felt and perceived but *beyond it?*'[49] In the retreats of the last ten years of his life, he writes of his 'vertigo of fragility, of instability',[50] of his 'physical anxiety',[51] and of the rise of the 'old fear: that there is Nothing on the other side'.[52]

The fear of death as a possible dead end is almost never absent from the meditation notes on death from Teilhard's last ten retreats. But the fear is on the surface; deeper, and expressed much more often and more strongly, is an unshakeable faith and trust in God. In 1944, Teilhard begins his retreat journal by writing: 'Alone in retreat; alone at death; God has to be faced center to Center, person to Person . . . *Usque ad senec-tatem et senium ne derelinquas me, Domine.* Certainly, from year to year, *advesperascit,* and quickly.'[53] The seventh day of the same retreat is set aside for medita-tion on the cross; and he writes, 'The difficult thing, in old age, is to accommodate oneself to the interior per-spective of a life *without a future* for oneself. (Face to the wall.) And yet, so many immediate interests tend to evaporate, . . . a superior interest is necessary to bind them together.'[54] In his 1945 retreat, he entitles the seventh day, 'Redemption, day of diminution undergone in communion' and makes this entry: 'To accept, to love, interior fragility, and age, with the shadows and the spaces ahead always shorter.'[55] In 1946, the notes for the day of meditation on the cross are brief: 'To love: Decline, and Life in spite of Decline; communion with Diminution *and* with chance animated by the christic influence.'[56] The 1948 retreat speaks of 'communion through death'.[57] Finally, in his last retreat, in 1954, he notes: 'Seventh Day — Cross. . . . Communion with: Senescence; Diminution. *Appropinquat hora Christi.*'[58] In the end, the dominating meaning of the cross is that it is a passage through death to Jesus Christ.

3

TOWARDS A THEOLOGY OF THE CROSS
Gerald O'Collins, S.J.

In the 1960s Jürgen Moltmann's *Theology of Hope*[1] triggered off a new phase of theological reflection. A decade later his *The Crucified God*[2] helped to initiate a fresh look at the place of Christ's cross in christian thought and life. While this book still provokes us, it seems worth asking: What themes should we expect any adequate theology of the cross to incorporate? How can we assess our theological versions of Good Friday to be reliable and not just loose talk of our own making?

This chapter aims at nominating some major requirements for a theology of the cross. It will present a case without arguing everything out in detail. These requirements emerge from an examination of three topics: (1) the prolegomena to any discussion of Good Friday, (2) the crucifixion itself, and (3) our response to that event. Let us take up these topics in turn.

The Prolegomena

'Prolegomena' might not look the most useful word

to employ here. Should we rather speak of 'the conditions for the possibility of a theology of the cross'? Both expressions, however, take serious and obvious risks. The prolegomena to any enquiry will determine not just what we go on to say but what we feel no need to say. Essential elements which do in fact belong to some theme may then find no place in our final statement. Likewise, by listing at the outset the 'conditions for the possibility' of studying some theme in an organized way, we could unwittingly dispense in advance with conditions that genuinely apply to our study and possibilities that are actually realized in our theme. This danger becomes most acute when we turn to 'Christ crucified, a stumbling block to Jews and folly to Gentiles' (I Cor 1:23).

The incarnation remains a mystery which eludes the grasp of the bravest Chalcedonian and post-Chalcedonian christologies. Yet St Paul felt at liberty to affirm the incarnation without too much fuss: 'When the time had fully come, God sent forth his Son, born of a woman. born under the law' (Gal 4:4). The real 'scandal' for the apostle was the cross. This pauline conviction should check any overly optimistic views about a scholarly progress which would now allow us to nominate easily 'the prolegomena to', or 'the conditions for the possibility of', even some modest theology of the cross.

All these misgivings should not, however, encourage the impossible attempt to reflect on Good Friday while systematically excluding all preliminary convictions. A presuppositionless theology of the cross would be an illusion. What we need is not the pretence of being utterly 'open-minded', but rather the willingness to let our prolegomena be called into question, adjusted and qualified in the light of our subsequent ponderings on the cross.

All that said, let me suggest three areas where convictions should be clarified before tackling Good

Friday and the events surrounding it. We need preliminary theories about (a) God, (b) evil and (c) atonement which will allow us to press ahead and shape a theology of the cross.

First of all, God. Any theology of the cross requires a view of God which looks beyond creation, incarnation, resurrection and second coming to imagine a God whose revelation and redemption could take place through a crucifixion — the last event in the world where we would expect to find such a revelation and redemption. To take two examples. Those who applaud the book as well as those who lament it recognize where the theological center of John Robinson's *Human Face of God* lies: back at the creation. He makes evolving creation the primary mystery and insists that Jesus was 'with the rest of us, a genuine product of the evolutionary process'. The stardust at the foundation of the world prepared the way for the coming of Jesus.[3] The Teilhardian perspective of a creating God — or rather a particular version of such a perspective — dominates the book. It is not surprising that Calvary is bypassed to the point that neither 'cross' nor 'crucifixion' appear in the index. Such a theory of God built around creation cannot make anything of the fact that the human face of God became disfigured and silent on Good Friday. Here Moltmann's *The Crucified God* establishes its superiority. His notion of a *revelatio in contrariis* —- and, we might add, a *redemptio in contrariis* — allows him to appreciate Calvary.[4] The place where atheists say that belief in God ends is acknowledged to be the very place where divine revelation and salvation reach their climax. So far from its being an embarrassment, Moltmann appreciates the crucifixion as *the* event which reveals the triune God.

Before launching into a theology of the cross we need also (b) a theory of evil and sin which reckons with the lostness of man and his world. If we are to unravel even a little how the crucifixion saves men and women, we must take time out to ask at depth: What keeps the question of salvation alive today? What is the present reality and profound mystery of evil from which human kind yearns to be liberated? St Paul cannot produce a theology of the cross without also fashioning a theology of sin and evil. His classic work explains how sin has come into the world and enslaved human beings (Rom 5:12; 6:17ff). Death symbolizes and reveals man's lostness and sin (Rom 6:23). Paul's doctrine of sin and evil allows him to develop a theology of the cross which reaches its climax in the questions: 'If God is for us, who is against us? He who did not spare his own Son but gave him up for us all, will he not also give us all things with him?' (Rom 8:31f).

Two contemporary theologians (Bernard Lonergan and Wolfhart Pannenberg) illustrate how some theory of evil and sin is needed before we can get on with theological reflections on the crucifixion. In *Insight* Lonergan analyzes 'physical evil', 'moral evil' and 'basic sin'. This analysis of human development and decline lays the ground for his approach to redemption and the *Lex Crucis*.[5] Pannenberg, however, proves less successful in handling the saving consequences of Calvary. The strength of his theology is found elsewhere — in his sophisticated account of revelation and all that such a revelational theology involves. He has had little to say about human liberation from evil and sin. Early in his theological career he admitted his concentration on revelation but felt untroubled by it.

> The correlation of revelation and salvation cannot be discussed in detail here, since we are primarily concerned with the fundamental structure of revelation. However, the fact of this connection is presupposed throughout . . . For the man who is disposed to an openness toward God, revelation in its deepest sense means sal-

vation, fulfillment of his destiny and his very
being . . . The revelation of God truly speaks
to the sinner.[6]

More recently Pannenberg has recognized at this point
a gap in his theology: 'The role played by sin, evil,
suffering, destruction and brokenness in human history
has not received very extensive treatment in my writing.'[7]
This gap partly explains why he does not cope quite
satisfactorily with the redemptive impact of the crucifixion. One important condition for the possibility of
a theology of the cross is so far missing in Pannenberg's
writings.

Some theory of atonement forms (c) the third major
condition for theological reflection on the crucifixion. We
need a theory which will allow us to make sense of
the pauline 'he died for our sins'. How is it possible
that someone else should die for our sins? What could
such a representative death be expected to do? Are we
simply dealing with an innate but unjustifiable drive to
compensate in some way for sin and take away our
guilt feelings? In *The Calvary Christ* I expressed dismay
over the monstrous version of God and man that some
views of the atonement entail before developing a position
on reparation for objective guilt.[8] But does such an
approach continue to make atonement a matter of justice
and fail to respect God's loving mercy? The Prodigal
Son plans to ask, 'Treat me as one of your hired
servants' (Lk 15:19). But his father does not let him
expiate his sins by humiliating himself in that way. At
any rate, however we frame our theory, we need to
develop some reflections on atonement if we are to fashion
a full theology of the cross.

While fashioning a theory of atonement, we need to
'watch our language'. Some theologians can show themselves heedless of linguistic niceties when it comes to
dealing with Christ's precise role in making amends for

human sin. Words like 'representative', 'substitute' and 'solidarity' often fall into careless hands. James Dunn rightly sees the difficulties in such a term as 'substitution': 'It is too one-sided a concept; and it is too narrow in its connotation.' First, it is one-sided inasmuch as it conjures up 'pagan ideas of Jesus' standing in man's place and pleading with an angry God . . . "Substitution" does not give sufficient prominence to the point of primary significance — that God was the subject . . . God was in Christ reconciling the world to himself.' Second, ' "substitution" is also too narrow a word. It smacks too much of individualism to represent Paul's thought adequately."[9] Dunn's choice of topic ('Paul's Understanding of the Death of Jesus') makes him adhere rather closely to the apostle and his theology. One could have attempted a more radical critique of 'substitution' language. In a recent article I contrasted the roles of representative and substitute.

A decade ago critics took issue with Pannenberg for the carelessness he showed in explaining how Christ was our 'penal substitute'. If someone genuinely represents me, I must agree to his doing so and he must freely undertake the task. Representation is voluntary on both sides, as well as being restricted to specific areas and limited periods of time. A substitute, however, may be simply put in the place of another person or thing. Thus we can substitute a pawn for a castle on a chess-board. Another footballer may serve as substitute for a player injured on his way to a match. On the field the substitute takes the place of the injured man, who may be unconscious and hence does not know that someone is acting in his place. In wartime another prisoner may be shot in place of one who has escaped. There should be no need to pile up further examples to illustrate the

point. In the case of substitution between per-
sons, the parties concerned may neither know
nor be willing that the substitution takes place.
There is less intentionality and more passivity
apparent in the way we use the language of
'substitution'. This consideration alone should
win support for speaking of 'Christ our representative' and not of 'Christ our substitute'.[10]

This kind of critique does not concern itself directly with
the language of Paul or any other New Testament author
but rather with the wider question: What are the genuine
possibilities of using 'representation', 'substitution' or
similar terms in any theology of Jesus' atoning death?

The Crucifixion Itself

My first set of requirements touched three major
prolegomena for a theology of the cross. Let me now
turn to the crucifixion itself. Here any adequate theological account ought to respect three items: the inter-
relationship between the crucifixion and other christological mysteries, the freedom of *all* the agents involved,
and the symbolic-mythical qualities of the cross.

(a) First of all, any theology of the cross would
remain patently inadequate if it neglected to relate the
event of Calvary both backwards to the christological
mysteries of creation, the call and sufferings of God's
people, the incarnation and ministry of Jesus, *and* forwards to the resurrection, the coming of the Holy Spirit
and the *parousia*. A couple of examples can serve to
illustrate success or failure in meeting this requirement.
Hans Küng like others helpfully emphasizes how Jesus
passed from his ministry to his death because he remained
faithful to a vocation and a message which entailed a
striking solidarity with the lost, the godless, and the
alienated of his society. The physician who came to call
and cure the unrighteous went to die as their representa-

tive. Küng successfully relates Calvary back to the ministry by calling attention to Jesus' commitment to those who were obviously and openly guilty. A willingness to associate with tax agents, prostitutes and other groups considered undesirable by the 'good' people helped to put Jesus on the cross.[11]

There are, of course, different ways of relating the ministry and crucifixion of Jesus. Thus Pannenberg singles out Jesus' claim to authority which the events of the passion called into question. Nevertheless, a ministry to the reprobate which ended in a shameful death between two reprobates is a clear way of linking the ministry to Calvary.

Moltmann also picks up this link between the ministry and the crucifixion in his *The Crucified God*.[12] We can spot here an interesting shift in his interests. More than a decade ago many theology watchers called his *Theology of Hope* the most important work in its field from the 1960s. That book introduced the death and resurrection of Jesus with a lengthy discussion of Old Testament material. (Some critics even maintained that this concern with Israel's history of promise so established Moltmann's case that the story of Jesus became a mere appendix to the argument.) But then that book hardly made a passing nod at Jesus' ministry, as it swept from the Jewish background to the passion. In *The Crucified God* lines are drawn between the ministry and the death of Jesus. Moltmann also takes up the later sufferings of the Jewish people to write a theology that is unmistakably post-Auschwitz. However, no firm lines are established between the fate of Jesus and the earlier suffering history (*Leidensgeschichte*) of God's people.[13] *Leidensgeschichte* emerges as a favorite term in *The Crucified God*. Nevertheless, this book does not follow the example of Moltmann's earlier classic by sufficiently linking the events of Good Friday and Easter Sunday back to the suffering history of Israel.

37

The basis for interpreting Calvary remains perhaps a little narrow. We may not forget how the cross casts its shadow before it in the Babylonian Captivity, the story of Job, Isaiah's portrayal of the Suffering Servant and other elements in Israel's *Leidensgeschichte*.

In *The Crucified God* Moltmann has some peculiarly happy ways of relating the crucifixion *forwards* to the resurrection. He reverses Bultmann's notorious dictum to declare: 'Christ's death on the cross . . . expresses the significance of his resurrection for us and not vice versa . . . It is not his resurrection that shows that his death on the cross took place "for us", but on the contrary, it is his death on the cross "for us" that makes relevant his resurrection "before us".'[14] All in all, *The Crucified God* is possibly more successful at linking the crucifixion forwards not only to the resurrection, but also to the life of the Church, the history of the Jewish people and the *parousia*.

(b)   Second, any theology of the cross should respect the lovingly exercized *freedom* of Jesus and his Father, as well as the misused freedom of Pilate, Caiaphas and the other human beings who brought about the crucifixion. It will, of course, prove thoroughly difficult to relate the free choices of all the agents involved in the death on Calvary and see, as it were, how this 'triple causality' interacts. Nevertheless, it is a false move to minimize the liberty of one or other of these agents, especially Jesus. Wolfhart Pannenberg has gone as far as any recent theologians in playing down the voluntary obedience of Jesus. The way he explains matters, Jesus was so seized by his mission that he was not left with any genuinely human choice about accepting or refusing his death on Calvary.[15] However, this flies in the face of the Gospel evidence, as well as creating severe theological difficulties. Pannenberg ignores, for instance, the agony in the garden. Theologically, if we deny or neglect Jesus' free purposes, we turn him into a passive victim whose murder God picked to serve for the salvation of mankind. Karl Rahner in his celebrated 1951 article on Christology rightly insisted that the redemption was truly and intrinsically an act of human freedom.[16] Otherwise, we risk changing the crucifixion into an episode that did not properly belong to history.

To use Leopold von Ranke's term, Calvary was par excellence a 'scene of freedom', where deliberately chosen actions decisively affected human history. A set of free decisions made this event supremely significant. Ranke saw freedom as 'combined with power', a theme to which we return in a moment.[17] The point here is simply to emphasize that a theology of the cross has to reckon with the full range of freedom involved in the crucifixion being *both* an act of God *and* an act of man. We dare not suppress any of St Paul's affirmations: when he points to the agents involved: a group of human beings (I Thess 2:15), Jesus himself (Gal 2:20) and God the Father (Rom 8:32).

(c) In the third place, a theology of the cross needs to reflect on the *symbolic* values of the crucifixion. The introduction to Moltmann's *The Crucified God* ended as follows:

> In front of me hangs Marc Chagall's picture *Crucifixion in Yellow*. It shows the figure of the crucified Christ in an apocalyptic situation: people sinking into the sea, people homeless and in flight, and yellow fire blazing in the background. And with the crucified Christ there appears the angel with the trumpet and the open roll of the book of life. This picture has accompanied me for a long time. It symbolizes the cross on the horizon of the world, and can be thought of as a symbolic expression of the studies which follow. A symbol invites thought

(P. Ricoeur). The symbol of the cross invites rethinking.[18]

This final paragraph of the introduction led me to expect what I did not find — a discussion of the values and meanings symbolically communicated by the cross. At the beginning of chapter two a few things are said about the symbol of the cross which 'invite thought'. But that is about all. *The Crucified God* establishes its superiority in other ways.

The Cross Misused

If Moltmann fails to meet some expectations, at least he does not contribute to long-standing misuses of the cross as symbol. I am not thinking here simply or even primarily of the cross being reduced to the status of a rich ornament. Then it functions to complement colors and patterns, to express a bishop's power and wealth, to enhance the beauty of a neck on which it dangles, or even to act as a thinly veiled sex symbol. What has looked ugly ever since the fourth century has been the use of Christ's cross to symbolize political and military power and success.

The vision of the Emperor Constantine left its particular and dangerous scar on the christian memory. Before he accepted the christian faith Constantine had shown himself a keen devotee of Victory, a divinity with an altar on the Capitoline hill. After his 'conversion' Constantine interpreted military success as the gift, no longer of a goddess, but of the crucified Christ. His soldiers wore the cross on their helmets and shields. The promise ('*in hoc signo vinces,* in this sign you will conquer') came true repeatedly.

After Constantine's mother made her discovery in Jerusalem, the distribution of fragments of the true cross came to play a part in international affairs. Bruce Harbert summarizes some of the evidence:

> Relics of the cross were seen as a potent protection in time of war. During the siege of Rome by the Lombards in 756 a procession of supplication was held in which a relic of the cross was carried round the city with the treaty that the Lombards had violated fixed to it. When the emperor Mauritius made his expedition to Thrace in 593, the Byzantine army set out led by a golden lance in which was set a piece of the cross. In 622, Heraclius took a relic of the cross with him when he set out on a military expedition against Persia. In 864 Pope Nicholas I took with him a relic of the cross when he went out to confront the troops of Louis II. Charlemagne used to carry with him into war a reliquary containing a fragment of the cross . . . Asser tells us that Alfred himself took relics with him wherever he went. The possession of a relic of the cross seems to have been seen almost as a sign of royal power.[19]

We may dismiss the follies of our christian forebears who misused the cross as their secret weapon for military success and slaughter. Of course, the cross of Christ was never meant to signify *that kind* of victory. But I wonder whether the old conviction ('the cross is on our side') is truly dead. The Venerable Bede attributed St Oswald's triumph over the Welsh invaders at Hexham to the wooden cross around which Oswald (like Constantine a new convert to Christianity) and his Northumbrians made their stand. In a recent book Dr Gordon Huelin felt free to endorse Bede's conviction:

> The Venerable Bede . . . tells us of the rough wooden cross put together in the utmost haste . . . and of the devout Oswald in all the ardour

of his newly-found faith grasping the Christian standard with both hands and holding it upright while his soldiers heaped the earth around it until at last it was firmly fixed in the ground. With the light of dawn, the forces of Cadwallon came down like waves; but they broke in vain against the rock of that cross 'towering o'er the wrecks of time'. Oswald's prayer was answered, and the tyrant and his army were utterly routed by the defenders of the faith. The rough wooden cross so hastily set up had decided the fate of Britain.[20]

I shrink from making comments that could be construed as another example of those petty and spiteful debates among theologians. But we all need to put two questions to our consciences. Do we continue to look on our crucified Savior as the strong God who will win our battles *now* and lead us to earthly victory and success? Have we turned even his cross into an idol that guarantees our triumph in some latterday crusade?

Talk about 'killing a Moslem or a Commie for Christ' may have become less frequent. But little hints of that spirit still pop up disconcertingly. Does this stanza of *America the Beautiful* use the cross to promise a peace which will come under the flag of 'our' military might?

Lift high the cross, unfurl the flag,
May they forever stand
United in our hearts and hopes,
God and our native land.
America, America, may God thy love increase
Till wars are past, and earth at last,
May follow Christ in peace.

Let me hasten to add that taking the cross to express and effect worldly power is a very different thing from using images of battle to interpret Calvary. The ancient Latin hymns of the Church reach for the language of military engagements as they recall the Lord's death. One thinks of the hymns with which Venantius Fortunatus celebrated the coming of the relics of the cross to Poitiers (*Vexilla regis prodeunt; Fulget crucis mysterium;* and *Pange, lingua, gloriosi proelium certaminis*), as well as of the *Victimae Paschali.* This magnificent sequence shows 'death and life' fighting an 'extraordinary conflict (*mors et vita duello conflixere mirando*)'. In the Anglo-Saxon religious poem, *The Dream of the Rood,* and other medieval works, Christ appears not as victim or martyr but as an heroic warrior whose endurance wins the day. At terrible cost to himself, Christ the Champion gains his victory, despite the apparent defeat of the crucifixion. But this paradox of real victory in seeming defeat is a far cry from misusing the cross to symbolize and guarantee earthly success 'in our time'.[21]

If we refuse to pervert the cross into an expression of this-worldly power, what ways does its symbolism take us? We can only answer cautiously here. Symbols are felt to be important before we consciously perceive their possible meanings. Even when we 'explain' them, we should know that our explanations can never hope to exhaust the rich range of meaning that is present. Besides, different people will recognize different meanings.

That said, we may identify two sides to the symbolism of the cross. It represents *both* degradation *and* order, *both* destruction *and* redemption.

The masters of Jesus' world regularly used crucifixion to execute runaway slaves and rebels. Not everyone who looks today at a cross or crucifix cares to think of the ancient Romans as sadists who liked to degrade people and inflict frightful cruelties with sheer delight. Nevertheless, crucifixion happened within the regular framework of their society. Milan Machovec rightly insists that crucifixion gets close to being unbearable in its horror: 'The torments accompanying the death agony in this form of execution were extreme.'[22] A man pinned on a cross symbolizes the weakness of unspeakable pain, an extreme and shameful case among pointless atrocities.

In pondering the degrading and destructive aspects of crucifixion we should allow for the range of meanings it suggested to Romans, Jews and Christians. J. B. Phillips' translation of Philippians 2:8 ('and the death he died was the death of a common criminal') obscures the significance of such a death for the Romans, not to mention any other group. For them Jesus died the death of 'an uncommon criminal', executed like one of the slaves crucified in the aftermath of Spartacus' uprising. For Jews a crucifixion — even more than hanging — conveyed a sense of godlessness, lawlessness and blasphemy. It suggested utter shame.

The horror generated by crucifixion gets minimized in a recent study by Barnabas Lindars. On the one hand, he acknowledges that on Calvary the death of Jesus was 'a shattering blow' which made it 'extremely difficult' for the disciples to interpret 'the death of such a righteous man' as 'his exaltation'. On the other hand, however, once 'the initial shock' was over, the disciples 'could search for a clue to God's will in the tragedy and come up with the conviction' of exaltation. Lindars assures us: 'The third day is *really just about long enough* for this process of reflection to have taken place and have led to a deep conviction.' I wonder how anyone could feel satisfied that — even without some objective experience of the risen Christ — 'the third day' would have been 'really just about long enough' after a crucifixion for close friends to cope with the shock and pass through a process of reflection to such a deep conviction. The physical and symbolic ugliness of crucifixion was such that it took Christians centuries before they could bring themselves to represent Jesus on the cross. One thinks too of the reactions of people who have witnessed atrocity killings in the twentieth century. All of this should make one much more cautious about maintaining that forty-eight hours would be 'really just about long enough' to cope in the way suggested with such a shock — even though in fact no 'objective experience' of resurrection 'acted as a catalyst' to convince the disciples of exaltation.

If degradation and destruction form one range of meanings, order and redemption gather up another set of meanings when we reflect on the symbolism of the cross. Various fathers of the Church, Thomas Aquinas, Jung and others have noted this second range of meaning. The cross expresses a totality and order which readily suggest universal redemption. The crucified Christ forms a kind of axis of the universe. He hangs impaled between heaven and earth, his body stretched out in four directions and his arms open to the world. Day by day people experience this symbolic power when they visit churches. Great crosses and crucifixes at the end of buildings instantly seize their attention and produce order within the space enclosed by walls and roof.

St Paul's theology matches this double-sided symbolism of the cross, when he speaks of 'power being made perfect in weakness' (2 Cor 12:9). The language of 'weakness' can easily lead us astray into thinking of moral weaknesses. For the apostle the crucifixion was the supreme example of 'weakness' (2 Cor 13:4) or 'vulnerability', as we might say. We catch his meaning by talking of order being made perfect in degrading disorder and redemption taking place in destruction. It sounds paradoxical. But this paradox parallels the peculiarly double-sided nature of the cross as symbol.

The Existential Correlate

Finally, we come to the human response in the face of the crucifixion. St Paul's theme of 'power in weakness' enjoys a prominent place in II Corinthians, the closest thing in his writings to an autobiography. In this letter the apostle meditates on his own suffering existence. The fact of Jesus' crucifixion remains central. But Paul does not fill out the picture by recalling the arrest, the trial, the scourging and other events in the passion. Rather he reflects on the lashings, betrayals, shipwrecks and other 'weaknesses' which have afflicted his apostolic mission:

> Five times I have received at the hands of the Jews the forty lashes less one. Three times I have been beaten with rods; once I was stoned. Three times I have been shipwrecked; a night and a day I have been adrift at sea; on frequent journeys, in danger from rivers, danger from robbers, danger from my own people, danger from Gentiles, danger in the city, danger in the wilderness, danger at sea, danger from false brethren; in toil and hardship, through many a sleepless night, in hunger and thirst, often without food, in cold and exposure (11:24-27).

St Paul feels drawn into the event of the crucifixion. He knows it is not possible to distinguish in any absolute way between that event and his own response to it. He cannot interpret Calvary without participating in it. This I call the 'existential correlate' of the crucifixion. The theme belongs to any adequate theology of the cross.

A theologian could take up the 'existential correlate' at two levels, the individual and the communitarian. First, he could explore the signals of the crucifixion in the lives of individual Christians and human beings. Such an approach could help to elucidate the answers coming in when someone asks: Where have I seen the cross in my existence? Where am I seeing the cross? Where will I see the cross? Second, a similar procedure applies to the life of the community. A genuine theology of the cross would call into question much talk about a 'successful'

Church, a 'well-run' diocese, a 'flourishing' congregation, a parish 'in good shape'. The christian community in its different groupings should be reminded of the principle, 'power made perfect in weakness'. Moltmann's *Church in the Power of the Spirit* rightly speaks of 'the community of the cross (*Kreuzgemeinde*)'. For the most part, however, ecclesiologies — or at least Roman Catholic ones — do not take up this theme. One normally looks in vain for a section or chapter entitled 'The Crucified Church' or 'The Church under the Shadow of the Cross'. But a theology which took its cue from St Paul would demand such reflections as part of a genuinely christian ecclesiology.

This chapter has aimed at nominating minimum requirements for a theology of the cross, and to clarify 'the word of the cross' (I Cor 1:18), following Maurizio Flick's nominated requirements in chapter one and the approach to the cross of Teilhard de Chardin explained by Robert Faricy in chapter two. In the following chapter, Robert Faricy expands on the necessary components of a theology of the cross.

4

THE CROSS IN CONTEXT

Robert Faricy, S.J.

Gerald O'Collins gives us a useful tool, a kind of trellis on which to stretch out Teilhard de Chardin's theology of the cross, a conceptual grid to lay down on top of Teilhard's thought so as to analyze it and to comment on it. He lists the necessary components of a theology of the cross: (1) the prolegomena, (2) a consideration of the crucifixion as fact and as symbol, (3) our existential response to that event. I would like to begin by looking at Teilhard's theology of the cross according to Gerald O'Collins' 'three prolegomena' to any theology of the cross: preliminary theories about (a) God, (b) evil and (c) atonement.

The Prolegomena

What lies at the center of Teilhard's theology is not the mystery of the cross but the mystery of the parousia, of the second coming of Jesus. More exactly, at the heart of all Teilhard's religious thought is Jesus risen as he-who-is-to-come. Can the cross ever be the focus of theological interest? Yes, when the theology is one of christian life, looking at christian living here and now, for we are — as Jesus was — in the structure of the cross. But when theology looks at Jesus Christ, who must finally be the center of all christian theological reflection, then the cross can no longer dominate; because Jesus is Lord, constituted Lord in and through his resurrection.

Too often theology has painted itself into a corner by choosing a 'theology of the cross' rather than a 'theology of creation'. But we have to choose both at once. Early in the first centuries of Christianity, the pauline idea of 'creation in Christ' (Col 1:16) began to be lost. Creation was assigned to the Father, partly through the influence of the creeds ('I believe in one God, the Father almighty, creator of heaven and earth'), and redemption to the Son. Creation and Christ were no longer associated intimately, and creation and redemption, which for Paul and Irenaeus and Justin were aspects of one process of pleromization in Christ, came apart and became 'the order of creation' and 'the order of redemption'. The separation turned into a divorce with the Roman Catholic distinction between man's 'natural' and 'supernatural' finalities (Cajetan and Suarez) and with the theology of the two kingdoms (Luther). And so theology lost the concept of the lordship of Jesus. The creation-redemption split has been further maintained in our own time, on the Protestant side by confessionally-oriented exegetical options, stressing faith, law and gospel, sin and redemption, neglecting the so important creation and royal theologies. And also in Roman Catholicism: Henri de Lubac and Karl Rahner have put nature and supernature back together, but only at the level of *personal* existence, leaving a split-level theological world view, divided between creation and redemption and finding it impossible to focus on Jesus as Lord. All this has much to do with Gerald O'Collins' first pro-

49

legomenon to a theology of the cross: a theory about God.

(a)   Teilhard de Chardin's theology of God is a theology of Jesus as the future, final, focal point of the world's convergence, a theology of Jesus as Lord understood in the perspective of a world in evolution. He puts Jesus back into God and back into creation without, of course, taking him out of redemption. Teilhard's synthesis is flimsy and frail, but it holds together because it stands on the Cappodocians, on Irenaeus, on Paul, and — for that matter — on Jesus' use of the first few verses of Psalm 110: 'The Lord said to my Lord, sit at my right hand until I make your enemies a footstool.'

(b)   The second prolegomenon to a theology of the cross, a theory of evil, is present in Teilhard's religious thought. He sees evil as a dimension of this-world reality. Teilhard does not entirely underestimate evil in the world because he has a theology of Jesus' lordship. In christian theology, a strong appreciation of Jesus' dominion and power is needed to balance any truly serious appreciation of sin, of the devil, of the structural (ideological, socioeconomic, material) forces of evil in the world. Evil can be seen as an all-permeating dimension of history (personal as well as collective) only when Jesus is seen as Lord. If evil is faced squarely in all its impressive and destructive power, then the idea of an all-powerful God who has universal dominion is threatened. Therefore, only a theology with a strong concept of the omnipotence and the universality of Jesus' lordship can take at all seriously the presence of evil in this world. Otherwise evil looms as strong as God, and the picture becomes that of Manicheism: an evil force and a good force (divine), equal or nearly equal, pitted against each other.

(c)   The third prolegomenon for a theology of the cross is a theory of atonement. Teilhard's theology of atonement is one of reconciliation, of unification, of 'at-one-ment'. Evil is divisive, and it is overcome through unification bonded by love. In this way, Jesus' act of the cross makes reparation for sin: it unifies, 'repairs' the world by uniting its parts.

The Crucifixion Itself and the Cross as Symbol

Surely, the crucifixion must be taken seriously as a concrete historical event. I do not, however, believe that details are necessary; there seems no need (utility perhaps, and inspiration, but not need) to dwell on the horribleness of what happened. Paul, again, is the model; the crucifixion stands — 'I preach Jesus Christ, and him crucified' — in all its mind-boggling historicity. But, for Paul, as for Teilhard, it is the risen Lord who is central.

But what about symbolic uses and misuses of the cross? How one takes the symbolic possibilities of the cross depends on how one construes the christian doctrine of the lordship of Jesus; and that, in turn, is tied up with how one relates creation and redemption. When creation and redemption are separated, then the cross — seen as only in the order of redemption — becomes an almost purely negative symbol. It can be understood as ordered to Jesus' own resurrection, because historically that is what happened. But the causality of the death of Jesus regarding the new creation and the final end-time transformation is inevitably missed. If the connection between cross and creation is missed, so will be missed the causal connection between the cross and the new creation. By new creation, of course, I am not referring only to grace and justification, but also to the world to come. Jesus recreates, reconciles, all things through his cross. 'For in him all the fullness of God was pleased to dwell, and through him to reconcile to himself all things, whether on earth or in heaven, making peace by the blood of his cross' (Col 1:19-20).

Roman Catholic symbolism relating to the cross has

always been basically positive except where it has deviated from its authentic forms. The devotion to the Precious Blood understands the blood Jesus shed on the cross not only as expiation for sin but as nourishing and life-giving. The devotion to the Sacred Heart, pierced by a lance, centers on the love of Jesus Christ and on the christian possibility of making reparation (a positive contribution) to Jesus' heart. The Stations of the Cross underline the fact that Jesus, by his cross, has saved the world. An interesting question: Why has Roman Catholic theology neglected these devotions? It is nearly a contemporary cliché that theology today reflects on experience. Why then has Roman Catholic theology, with a few exceptions, notably Karl Rahner's writings on the Sacred Heart, failed to reflect on those religious experiences represented in Roman Catholic piety by the devotions to the Precious Blood, the Sacred Heart, and the Stations of the Cross? I would like to suggest an answer.

Because the orders of creation and redemption remain to some extent separated in the Roman Catholic as well as in the Protestant tradition, and because this separation weakens theologically the bond between creation and cross, and because in consequence the lordship of Jesus and creation in Christ have been greatly neglected as theological concepts, therefore the act of Jesus on the cross cannot be understood theologically as a positive act that saved the world (and not just 'souls'). As a result, all symbolism that contains, symbolically, this content — that Jesus by his death on the cross positively saved the world — escapes contemporary theological reflection. Theology, dividing creation and cross, unable to see how the cross saved all creation, has nothing to say about symbols that have for content precisely that Jesus through his Cross has saved all creation. It is not theological snobbism that keeps reflection on popular forms of piety such as the devotions to the Precious Blood, the Sacred Heart, and the Stations of the Cross out of the theological literature and out of the seminary courses on redemption. It is theological failure to know how to reflect on these experiences; a failure resulting from, still today, failing to see the world in one christocentric perspective in which creation and redemption are united in Jesus Christ.

And this is why, so often in theology, the cross cannot be appreciated as a symbol of victory. Of course, the cross in its positive symbolism, as a symbol of victory over evil, can be abused. But abuses do not invalidate the whole christian tradition of the victory of the cross, of the cross as representing victory over sin and over everything that oppresses us.

The weakness of Teilhard's theology of the cross, it seems to me, lies here. He does not pay sufficient attention to the victory of the cross of Jesus. True, he underlines the 'victory' aspect much more than most contemporary theologians. But, in my opinion, Teilhard, along with most theology since his death in 1955, does not sufficiently stress the *power* of the cross. Correspondingly, although he faces evil better than most contemporary theologians, he fails in the end to adequately point out the force of evil in the world, including that evil entity that we call Satan, the devil.

This does not appear to be the place to enter into a discussion of the existence, meaning, and function of the devil. Let it suffice to comment briefly on the fact that theology today hardly knows what to do with the devil, and so writes him off as a myth, a personification of dark (personal and social) psychological drives. It is only when both the lordship of Jesus and the power of his victory on the cross are adequately put into relief that theology is free to deal seriously with evil in the world. Without sufficient emphasis on the power and dominion of Jesus' lordship, the danger of Manicheism prevents

— often unconsciously — serious consideration of the malice of sin and the existence of the devil.

The Existential Correlate

What does the cross mean for the Christian and for the Church in everyday life? For Teilhard de Chardin, the cross has a primary meaning as the symbol of the progress that is made through suffering and through difficult labor. I am changing somewhat Gerald O'Collins' notion of an existential correlate to Jesus' passion and death. I am taking it to mean not just the christian response to Jesus' cross, but that response seen as a voluntary participation in the cross through christian service in the world. This theme, christian service in the structure of the cross, is one of the predominant themes of Roman Catholic theology and official teaching in the past fifteen years. I would like to sketch briefly the main points of recent Catholic thought on service in the structure of the cross, and so situate Teilhard's theology of participation-in-the-cross-of-Jesus.

The influence of Teilhard's religious thought on the Second Vatican Council's Pastoral Constitution on the Church in the Modern World, *Gaudium et spes,* is well known. *Gaudium et spes* understands all reality as centered on Jesus Christ risen and as moving toward him as its Lord, its goal, and its future. The introduction states that Jesus Christ, who died and has risen, is 'the key, the focal point, and the goal of all human history' (no. 10). Later on, the document says: 'Jesus Christ is the goal of human history, the focal point of the longings of history and civilization, the center of the human race, the joy of every heart and the answer to all its yearnings' (Part I, chapter 4, no. 45). The same paragraph goes on to quote the New Testament regarding the Father's plan in Christ: 'To re-establish all things in Christ, both those in the heavens and those on earth' (Eph 1:10), and the words of the Lord, 'I am the Alpha and the Omega, the first and the last, the beginning and the end' (Rev 22:13). Human progress, then, is in continuity with the world to come, even though human freedom makes progress often ambiguous; earthly progress must be distinguished from the growth of God's kingdom, but it is of vital importance to the kingdom of God. 'For after we have obeyed the Lord, and in his Spirit nurtured on earth the values of human dignity, brotherhood and freedom, and indeed all the good fruits of our nature and enterprise, we will find them again, but freed of stain, burnished and transfigured. This will be so when Christ hands over to the Father a kingdom eternal and universal . . . On this earth that kingdom is already present in mystery. When the Lord returns it will be brought into full flower' (Part I, chapter 3, no. 39). And so 'it is clear that people are not deterred by the Christian message from building up the world, or impelled to neglect the welfare of others. They are, rather, more strictly bound to do these very things' (Part I, chapter 3, no. 34).

Gaudium et spes, while stressing our service in and to the world as the christian response to the world, does not stress the cross, and speaks little of sin. Both Teilhard de Chardin's theology and *Gaudium et spes* act as strong influences on Latin American liberation theology, which arose partly in reaction to what was felt as the 'europeanism' and over-optimism of both. The theology of liberation emphasizes the identification of Jesus with the oppressed (Phil 2:6-11), sinful social structures, and liberation from those structures. (The exodus is an often cited theme).

Liberation theology points out that an important part of the Church's service, like that of Jesus, has always been 'to bring the good news to the poor, to proclaim freedom to captives, . . . to set the downtrodden free' (Isaiah 61:1). *Gaudium et spes* declares that 'the Gospel announces and proclaims the freedom of the sons of God, and repudiates all the bondage which ultimately results from sin' (Part I, chapter 4, no. 41). And the Church herself, in communicating to all mankind the freedom and the salvation of Christ, is called to follow the same path as Jesus, who took the nature of a slave (Phil 2:6) and, being rich, became poor for our sakes (II Cor 8:9). 'Thus the Church . . . is not set up to seek earthly glory . . . She recognizes in the poor and the suffering the likeness of her Founder . . . She does all she can to relieve their need and in them she strives to serve Christ' (*Lumen Gentium,* chapter 1, no. 8).

'Latin American liberation theology arises out of an experience: the discovery of institutionalized violence and the dimensions of oppression' (P. Berryman, 'Latin American Liberation Theology', *Theological Studies,* 34, 1973, p. 364). The theology of liberation became a broad, coherent movement with its own clear identity at the Second General Conference of the Latin American Episcopate (CELAM) in Medellin, Colombia, in the fall of 1968. This meeting set the authoritative orientation for the Latin American Church. Medellin sought to interpret the Latin American signs of the times in the light of faith. What is christian freedom as described at Medellin and in post-Medellin liberation theology? Christian freedom is freedom in the Spirit, interior freedom, but this interior freedom is not unconnected with social, economic, and political freedom. On the contrary, the freedom that Christianity brings is freedom from sin, and sin is often found in the very structures of human society as well as in the hearts of men. Sin within the person has consequences in society, and so it comes about that situations arise which are objectively sinful even though perhaps involving no immediate subjective responsibility at the time that those situations exist. Sinful structures, social, economic, and political, do exist in society; they are objective states of sin. Situations of unjust distribution of wealth, of oppression of various kinds, of starvation, of homelessness, of inhuman living conditions; all these are sinful situations, conditions of institutionalized violence. It is, then, part of the Church's mission to condemn such objectively sinful societal structures, and to work toward overcoming them.

Latin American liberation theology seems to be in a state of decline since 1972 or 1973. For one thing, many of those engaged in the implementation of pastoral guidelines for liberation have become increasingly engaged in purely political activities that have little or no religious import; some have simply lost hope in the Church hierarchy and now either reject or ignore it. Further, it appears that many Latin American bishops have had second thoughts since Medellin. Pro-Medellin bishops seem increasingly isolated, and the fifth anniversary of Medellin was passed over in silence by CELAM, the organization of bishops. Finally, some have carried liberation theology to a kind of extreme, mixing it with various brands of Marxism, divesting it of what they consider its overly theological elements, and putting it in the service of leftist political movements. An example of this tendency is the movement called Christians for Socialism, which exists in Italy as well as in Latin America, and which is often at odds with official policies of Roman Catholic Church authorities.

At the same time, the overall effect of the theology of liberation worked out in Latin America has been immense, and its influence will be felt for a long time, especially in Latin America. The effect of liberation theology is already evident in the development of the Catholic Church's official teaching in recent years. There is an almost straight line from *Gaudium et spes,* which understands the Church as for-the-world, as a servant Church, to the 1974 synod of bishops, which speaks frankly in the vocabulary of liberation theology.

Pope Paul VI, in *Populorum Progressio* (1967), speaking of the Church's contribution to the development of man and of all men, says that what the Church has to give is primarily a *vision,* a global vision of man and of humanity. The real turning point in the development of the Church's teaching on her role in secular matters is Pope Paul's letter to Cardinal Roy, the president of the Pontifical Commission on Justice and Peace, in 1971. This letter, *Octogesima Adveniens,* underlines not only the vision that the Church has to give to society, but the action, the active role, of the Church in the secular world. Not only the Christian but the institutional Church has an important part in the liberation of man. A few months later, in the fall of 1971, Pope Paul approved the document *On Justice in the World* drawn up by the Synod of Bishops. It speaks of the rights of all men and of all peoples to development; of the fact that often economic, social, and political structures oppress man; and of the need for the Church to denounce injustice. It states that action for justice is a constitutive part of evangelization. Thus, the Church's mission includes, as an essential element, action for justice.

The 1974 Synod of Bishops did not produce the expected document on evangelization. However, at the close of the Synod, the bishops made an official declaration, brief but clear and strong. It stresses that the Church in its mission of evangelization, must announce 'the integral salvation of man, or his full liberation'; and it states the need for Church action to liberate men from unjust social and political conditions as well as from their personal sins and sinfulness. The most important ideas of this declaration were repeated by Pope Paul VI in late 1975 in his apostolic exhortation on evangelization, *Evangelii nuntiandi.*

In recent Roman Catholic Church teaching and theology, a certain imbalance has been remedied. The idea of service, of helping to further the kingdom of

God, has been given new meaning by being placed in a future-oriented and social perspective. The christian vocation has been seen as in the structure of the cross and in the service of the world. The line of development runs from Teilhard de Chardin through *Gaudium et spes* and liberation theology up to recent teaching in official Church documents.

There appears, still, serious neglect of the idea of the *power* of the Cross, of the power of Jesus Christ who is Lord by virtue of his victory over evil through his cross and resurrection. What is still missing in Roman Catholic theology of the cross is a strong sense of the power that is made perfect in weakness. One hopes that theology will see itself in the structure of the cross and, in a new phase beyond the neo-Pelagian hope in human power to free the poor and the oppressed, become humble. It could become a theology not of eloquence but of the power and the glory of the cross of Jesus Christ.

5

REFLECTING FURTHER
Gerald O'Collins, S.J.

This chapter has two main aims: (1) to clarify and enlarge a little my own contribution, and (2) to reflect briefly on Robert Faricy's presentation of Teilhard's theology of the cross.

1

On re-reading my chapter included above, I became uncomfortably aware that three points cried out for further clarification or development. It is not that one can hope to produce absolutely tight and tidy statements when dealing with the theology of the cross. But some adjustments and additions seem called for.

To begin with the 'prolegomena'. This is a dangerous term which could all too easily imply that in an independent way we could fashion and systematize convictions about *God*, *evil* and *atonement* before applying these to the theme of the cross. I shrink, however, from any suggestion that we could independently elaborate here a full and satisfying philosophy which we then use to interpret Jesus' crucifixion — perhaps slightly modifying our philosophy in the process.

A classical distinction which William Van Roo brought to my attention could help here: *ordo doctrinae* (the order of doctrine) and *ordo inventionis* (the order of discovery). 'Prolegomena' was *not* meant to indicate the order of discovery, as if we were dealing with a chronological process which entailed two steps: first, some complete systematic philosophy about God, evil and atonement and, then, an examination of Good Friday in the light of that philosophy. Rather we face here an *ordo doctrinae* that illustrates the well-traveled route of any theology which takes its activity to be 'faith seeking understanding'. We begin with faith in the crucified Christ, one who died brutally in a world where so often the innocent rather than the guilty suffer. Starting from that faith we reflect back in order to clarify our understanding of God, evil, and both the need and manner for repairing a damaged moral order. What does Calvary impel us to say about these topics? We can develop and organize some insights which we then use in returning to the cross itself. We thus arrange our material in an *ordo doctrinae* which moves back to Calvary, but not as if this sequence purported to be the *ordo inventionis*.

Before leaving the 'prolegomena', I want to emphasize again the need to reflect on evil in constructing a theology of the cross. A recent advertisement for *The Times* asked: 'How can you face the music if you don't know the score?' I suspect that a Scottish friend of mine was right when he explained the widespread and persistent unwillingness to take the cross as a theme: 'You can't produce a theology of the cross if you won't think about evil and sin.' Or to parody the advertisement: 'How can you face the serious music of the cross if you refuse to know the score of evil?' A theologian of the cross must hear not only Jesus' words on Calvary

('My God, my God, why hast thou abandoned me?')
but also the cries of Job and the lamentations of the
suffering psalmist. It is not that I wish to *reduce* the
theology of the cross to the problem of evil. Maurizio
Flick rightly warns us against that. Nevertheless, any
theology of the cross will force Good Friday to remain
an odd surd, if it refuses to see how that day belongs
within the whole history of human suffering and evil.

Secondly, since I wrote the chapter included above,
Luis Martínez-Fazio pointed out to me how successfully
some artists have achieved the goal that I listed as a
first requirement under 'The Crucifixion Itself': the de-
sirability of relating Calvary both 'backwards' and 'forwards'. The 'sarcophagi of the passion' (from the fourth
century), for instance, link the crucifixion back to the
Old Testament *both* through sacrificial themes (for
instance, the death of Abel and Abraham's willingness
to surrender the life of Isaac) *and* through the figure of
Job, the just man who — mysteriously — must suffer.
These sarcophagi also link Jesus' crucifixion forwards to
the triumph of the resurrection, as well as to the suffering
history of the Church. Repeatedly they portray the
deaths of Peter and Paul. These martyrs represent,
respectively, Jewish and Gentile Christianity — in other
words, the universal Church. Those fourth century
artists show a deep ecclesial sense of Calvary, something
which later theologians were to forget. We have here
yet another case where the artistic imagination grasps a
truth let slip by the rational mind.

This brings me to the third point: the 'signals of
the crucifixion' in the life of the Church. I remarked
above on the failure of most recent Roman Catholic
ecclesiologies to concern themselves directly with the
implications of Calvary for the Church. Few would
dispute that any teaching on the Church should be
subordinated to beliefs about Christ. But many who
write on the Church fail to let that central event, the

passion and death of Jesus, shape their thinking. They derive the structures and dimensions of the Church from other christological mysteries: for instance, from the ministry of Jesus, his resurrection, or the coming of the Holy Spirit. In his excellent study of modern ecclesiologies, both Protestant and Catholic, Avery Dulles reports on various models of the Church as institution, mystical communion, sacrament, herald and servant.[1] But in all this and the further material from the contemporary scene which he provides one misses an image of the Church that goes back through the Fathers to John's Gospel: *the Church born from the pierced side of Christ*. Whether they realized it or not, Catholic theologians for centuries kept alive the model of the Church as crucified, precisely because they kept that image of the Church's origin on Calvary. In his recent *The Church in the Power of the Spirit* Jürgen Moltmann sets the theologoumenon about the birth of the Church from the heart of the crucified Christ at the center of his ecclesiology and proceeds to derive some consequences from that theologoumenon. Here Moltmann looks back through Pius XII's *Mystici Corporis* to Sebastian Tromp's 1932 work, *De Nativitate Ecclesiae ex Corde Jesu in Cruce,* hardly a work one finds cited and approved in recent Catholic ecclesiologies.[2]

A great deal is at stake here. Ecclesiologies that attend to the ministry, the resurrection, Pentecost and the early decades of the Church's history—while studiously ignoring the passion and death of Jesus—risk setting up false or inadequate scales of success. Church communities may then measure themselves on such scales of success and find themselves wanting. By all means let us ask how the gifts of the Holy Spirit should be freely and responsibly used to build up the common life of the Church. Let us reflect too on whether the Church faithfully journeys towards that coming kingdom to which Jesus repeatedly bore witness in his ministry.

But we should also recall themes like suffering, failure, powerlessness and abandonment. A Church born from the side of the crucified Christ will bear in its body the marks of crucifixion. It is at our peril that we fail to ponder and include in our ecclesiologies that profound 'weakness' which we see in the crucified Christ (II Cor 13:4).

2

For decades now Teilhard de Chardin's writings have fascinated as well as disconcerted readers. He has prompted both misgivings and applause. Here I would like to share one misgiving about Teilhard's theology of the cross. Did he ultimately interpret the cross as symbolizing progress and its price?

Robert Faricy's article reports how for Teilhard 'Jesus on the cross' symbolized 'the labor of the centuries'. Even if Teilhard warned against 'Protestant' perversions of the meaning of the cross, he declared 'the true meaning of the cross' to be: 'Toward progress through effort'. Did this verge on a Puritan work ethic?

In a sense a good deal of what Teilhard said should be connected with the carrying of the cross rather than with the event of the crucifixion itself. He called for a commitment that would endure pain and continue the efforts needed to achieve 'progress made in hard labor and suffering'.

Of course, Jesus carried the cross not to a place of success, but to a place of cruel death and seeming failure. I cannot stop myself asking whether Teilhard's thought, with its tremendous sense of the risen Christ and his presence, fails to do justice to the horror and evil of the crucifixion, turning it into the mere shadow-side of the resurrection.

Nevertheless, it would be unfair to ignore what Teilhard wrote about the cross symbolizing 'the dark retrogressive side of the universe in genesis'. For him the cross was not just 'the symbol of progress and victory', but represented a 'progress and victory' won *both* through mistakes, disappointments and hard work *and* despite 'moral downfalls'. That part of Faricy's report on Teilhard should not be passed over lightly.

For years now commentators have been circling round Teilhard's ideas, turning them over and poking at them with various sticks. The ideas are still there—provokingly. Robert Faricy deserves our warm thanks for making available some further material on those ideas. His chapter can only help towards deciding for ourselves on those key questions in Teilhard's theology of the cross: Does that theology — in an unacceptable way — interpret Jesus' cross as the 'mere' price of progress? Or is it insisting that no act of human retrogression, not even the crucifixion of Jesus, can ultimately stop the movement towards the omega-point? And does Teilhard's theology of the cross make the suffering and death of Jesus seem less real? Or does it lead us to a closer personal relationship with Jesus and towards a more christian attitude toward the cross in our own lives?

NOTES

NOTES to M. Flick, 'The Birth of a Theology of the Cross':

1. Z. Alszeghy and M. Flick, *Sussidio bibliografico per una teologia della croce* (Rome, 1975).

2. H. Schüller and E. Frings Kammerichs, *Das Kreuz. Ein Versuch in unserer Welt zu leben und zu verstehen* (Mainz, 1973).

3. U. Hedinger, *Wider die Versöhnung Gottes mit dem Elend* (Zurich, 1972).

4. See the approach to the theology of the cross in P. R. Régamey, *La croix du Christ et celle du chrétien* (Paris, 1969).

5. Cf. the timely linking of the theology of sin with that of redemption in P. Grelot, *Péché originel et rédemption* (Paris, 1973).

6. Cf. *Il mito della pena,* ed. E. Castelli (Rome, 1967).

7. Significant for the 1940s is the article of L. Beirnaert, 'Péché et libération chrétienne chez saint-Paul', *Psyché* 3 (1948) pp. 429-440; for the 1950s the book of W. Daim, *Tiefenpsychologie und Erlösung* (Vienna, 1954); for the last decade the work of P. Ricoeur is fundamental, *Freud and Philosophy: an Essay on Interpretation,* tr. D. Savage (New Haven, 1970).

8. Cf. the proceedings of the ecumenical meeting held at Grafrath in October 1972: published in Italian as *Sulla teologie della croce* (Brescia, 1974).

9. W. von Loewenich, *Luther's Theology of the Cross,* tr. H. J. A. Bouman (Belfast, 1976).

10. See, for example, *Zum Verständnis des Todes. Stellungnahme des Theologischen Ausschusses und Beschluss der Synode der Evangelischen Kirche der Union* (Gütersloh, 1968).

11. K. Kitamori, *Theology of the Pain of God* (London, 1966).

12. Cf. J. Moltmann, *The Crucified God,* tr. R. A. Wilson and J. Bowden (London, 1974).

13. *Dei Verbum*, no. 19; tr. A. Flannery (ed.), *Vatican Council II* (Tenbury Wells, 1975) p. 761.

14. This approach has been accepted by Catholics, especially after its prudent presentation by P. Benoit, *The Passion and Resurrection of Jesus Christ,* tr. B. Weatherhead (London, 1969).

15. Cf. G. Schneider, *Die Passion Jesu nach den drei älteren Evangelien* (Munich, 1973).

16. See, for example, X. Léon-Dufour, "Passion," *DBS* 6 (1960) pp. 1419-1492.

17. Cf. L. Marin, *Sémiotique de la Passion* (Paris, 1971) and even more D. Dormeyer, *Die Passion Jesu als Verhaltensmodell* (Munster, 1974).

18. See, for example, L. Morris, *The Cross in the New Testament* (Grand Rapids, 1965); similar reservations are expressed by H. Schürmann, *Jesu ureigener Tod* (Freiburg, 1974).

19. F. Hahn et al., *Rückfrage nach Jesu* (Freiburg, 1974).

20. Cf. A. Dauer, *Die Passionsgeschichte im Johannesevangelium* (Munster, 1972); J. T. Forestel, *The Word of the Cross* (Rome, 1974).

21. A. Poppi, *Le parole di Gesú in croce* (Padua, 1974).

22. R. G. Bandas, *The Master-Idea of St Paul's Epistles or the Redemption* (Bruges, 1925); E. Käsemann, 'The Saving Significance of the Death of Jesus in Paul,' *Perspectives on Paul,* tr. M. Kohl (London,

1971) pp. 32-59; B. Rinaldi, *La presenza della croce nelle principali lettere di S. Paolo* (Varese, 1972).

23. As well as the works of E. Lohse, E. Lohmeyer and L. Ruppert, we should note also G. Bourbonnais, *Cristo servo di Jahve. Saggio di una lettura teologica della Bibbia* (Turin, 1970).

24. S. Lyonnet and L. Sabourin, *Sin, Redemption and Sacrifice* (Rome, 1970); J. Jeremias, *Der Opfertod Jesu Christi* (Stuttgart, 1963); V. Taylor, *Jesus and his Sacrifice* (London, 1955); L. Moraldi, 'Espiazione nell'Antico e nel Nuovo Testamento,' *Rivista Biblica* 9 (1961) pp. 289-304; 10 (1962) pp. 3-17.

25. See 'Kreuz,' etc. in *Lexikon der Christlichen Ikonografie* 2 (Freiburg, 1970), pp. 562-656.

26. Even today the study of G. Oggioni remains a good guide in this field: 'Il mistero della redenzione' *Problemi e Orientamenti di Teologia Dommatica,* (Milan, 1957) pp. 237-344.

27. Cf. the posthumous work of J. Rivière, *Le dogme de la Rédemption dans la théologie contemporaine* (Albi, 1948).

28. G. Aulen [*Christus Victor,* tr. A. G. Hebert (London: 1970)] distinguishes the classic and patristic idea (in which God is moved simply by a free love for man), the Latin idea (in which God makes satisfaction to his justice through the cross), and the more recent idea (in which, through Christ its head, humanity makes satisfaction to God).

29. Cf. von Loewenich, *op. cit.*

30. Cf. U. Asendorf, *Gekreuzigt und Auferstanden. Luthers Herausforderung an die moderne Christologie* (Hamburg, 1971).

31. Cf. G. Greshake, 'Der Wandel der Erlösungsvorstellungen in der Theologiegeschichte', *Erlösung und Emanzipation,* R. Affemann et al. (Freiburg, 1973) pp. 69-101.

32. H. Kessler, *Die theologische Bedeutung des Todes Jesu* (Dusseldorf, 1971).

33. N. Baumert, *Täglich sterben und auferstehen* (Munich, 1973); E. Güttgemans, *Der leidende Apostel und sein Herr* (Göttingen, 1966).

34. See, for example, S. Breton, *La mystique de la passion. Etude sur la doctrine spirituelle de S. Paul de la Croix* (Tournai, 1962).

35. G. Mainberger, *Jesus starb umsonst* (Freiburg, 1970).

36. Denzinger-Schönmetzer, *Enchiridion Symbolorum* etc. n. 1740.

37. The prologue to the *Summa Theologiae.*

38. *Breviloquium,* prologue, n. 6.

39. Among various such modern attempts we should recall the article of H. G. Koch, 'Kreuzestod und Kreuzestheologie', *Herder-Korrespondenz* 29 (1975) pp. 147-152.

40. Vatican II, *Gaudium et Spes,* n. 38; cf. M. Flick, 'La croce e il progresso,' *Presbyteri* 3 (1969) pp. 168-176.

41. This international congress was held in Rome, 13-18 October 1975. The proceedings have been published in three volumes *La Sapienza della Croce Oggi* (Turin, 1976).

NOTES to R. Faricy, 'Teilhard de Chardin's Theology of the Cross':

1. The first two-thirds of this article was delivered as a paper at the International Congress, 'La sapienza della croce oggi', Rome, October 1975.

2. Teilhard's best complete presentation of his theory of evolution is *Man's Place in Nature,* tr. R. Hague (London, 1966).

3. Tr. B. Wall, *et al.* (New York, 1960).

4. Revelation 21:4.

5. While reading W. Somerset Maugham's *The Razor's Edge,* Teilhard copied a few lines into a notebook he kept for his reading notes: 'I wanted to believe, but I could not believe in a god which was not better than the ordinary decent man' (unpublished reading notes, page 58, notebook II for 1945). For Teilhard, Christ is, while completely human, still—in a certain sense—as big as the world, because he is its keystone and its Prime Mover (*Le Christique,* unpublished essay written in 1955, p. 4); Teilhard believed that this is the God contemporary man is looking for.

6. 'The Sense of Man', in *Toward the Future,* tr. R. Hague (London, 1975) p. 34.

7. 'The Road of the West', in *ibid.,* p. 53.

8. 'My Universe', in *Science and Christ,* tr. R. Hague (London, 1968) pp. 60-61.

9. 'Christology and Evolution', in *Christianity and Evolution,* tr. R. Hague (London, 1971) p. 85.

10. Journal, vol. I (August 26, 1916—January 4, 1919), texte intégral publié par N. et K. Schmitz-Moormann (Paris, 1975) p. 68.

11. *Ibid.,* p. 82.

12. 'Introduction to the Christian Life', in *Christianity and Evolution*, p. 163.

13. 'Christianity and Evolution', *ibid.*, p. 181.

14. Unpublished letter, August 11, 1936.

15. Unpublished letter of May 21, 1952, to Francois Richard. Teilhard goes on to say that he 'absolutely refuses to admit that atheism is an organic part of Marxism: Marxism does not deny the *whole God,* but only the God of the Above, *in the measure that* this God seems incompatible with the God of the Forward. From this, there is a way of mutual understanding between the Christian and the Marxist *in the perspective* of a universe in a state of cosmogenesis (but only in such a universe).'

16. *Journal*, p. 190.

17. 'The Struggle Against the Multitude', in *Writings in Time of War,* tr. R. Hague (London, 1968) p. 107.

18. 'Cosmic Life', *ibid.*, p. 67.

19. 'Introduction to the Christian Life', in *Christianity and Evolution*, p. 163.

20. *Idem.*

21. *The Divine Milieu,* tr. B. Wall *et al.* (New York, 1960) pp. 101-104.

22. *Ibid.*, pp. 103-104.

23. *Ibid.*, p. 104.

24. In *Christianity and Evolution*, pp. 212-220.

25. *Ibid.*, 216.

26. Letter of September 18, 1948, to Rhoda de Terra, published in *Letters to Two Friends* (New York, 1968) p. 187.

27. Retreat notes, 1941, unpublished.

28. *Idem.*

29. Retreat notes, 1942, unpublished.

30. Letter of Good Friday, 1955, to Father Ravier in *Pierre Teilhard de Chardin: Lettres intimes* (Paris, 1974) pp. 465-466.

31. These three phases of christian personalization, which form the outline of much of *The Divine Milieu,* are to be found outlined concisely in the essay 'Reflections on Happiness', in *Toward the Future,* tr. R. Hague (London, 1975) pp. 117-120.

32. *The Divine Milieu*, p. 96.

33. *Ibid.*, p. 97.

34. H. de Lubac, S.J., 'Maurice Blondel et le Père Teilhard de Chardin, mémoires échangés en décembre 1919, présentés par H. de Lubac', *Archives de philosophie,* 24 (1961) pp. 123-156.

35. Notes from public debate, Jan. 21, 1947, Paris; unpublished.

36. *The Phenomenon of Man*, tr. B. Wall (New York, 1965) p. 312.

37. 'Operative Faith', in *Writings in Time of War*, p. 230.

38. *Journal*, p. 337; cf. pp. 164-167 and 183.

39. 'My Universe', in *Science and Christ,* p. 62.

40. *Ibid.,* p. 63.

41. *The Divine Milieu*, p. 88.

42. See J. Laberge, *Pierre Teilhard de Chardin et Ignace de Loyola* (Paris, 1973) pp. 165-173.

43. Retreat of 1939, unpublished.

44. Retreat of 1941, unpublished.

45. Retreat of 1943, unpublished.

46. Retreat of 1942, unpublished.

47. Retreat of 1939, unpublished.

48. Retreat of 1941, unpublished.

49. Retreat of 1942, unpublished.

50. Retreat of 1945, unpublished.

51. *Idem.*

52. Retreat of 1949, unpublished.

53. Retreat of 1944, unpublished.

54. *Idem.*

55. Retreat notes, 1945, unpublished.

56. Retreat notes, 1946, unpublished.

57. Retreat notes, 1948, unpublished.

58. Retreat notes, 1954, unpublished.

NOTES to G. O'Collins, 'Towards a Theology of the Cross':

1. Tr. J. W. Leitch (London, 1967).

2. Tr. R. A. Wilson and J. Bowden (London, 1974).

3. (London, 1973) p. 148.

4. Pp. 25-28.

5. *Insight* (New York, 1957) pp. 666ff.; *De Verbo Incarnato* (Rome, 1964) pp. 552ff.; *A Second Collection* (London, 1974) pp. 7f., 271f.; *Method in Theology* (London, 1972) pp. 243f., 288. I owe these references to John Humphreys, S.J.

6. *Revelation as History,* tr. D. Granskou and D. Quinn (London, 1969) p. 156, fn. 14. The German original appeared first in 1961.

7. Postscript to E. Frank Tupper, *The Theology of Wolfhart Pannenberg* (London, 1974) p. 303.

8. (London, 1977) pp. 93ff.; see also pp. 106ff.

9. 'Paul's Understanding of the Death of Jesus', *Reconciliation and Hope,* ed. R. Banks (Exeter, 1974) pp. 125-141.

10. 'Jesus in Current Theology: II, Salvation and Commitment', *The Way* 17 (1977) p. 56.

11. *On Being a Christian,* tr. E. Quinn (London, 1977) pp. 266ff.

12. pp. 126ff.

13. But see *ibid.*, pp. 98ff., 270ff.

14. *Ibid.,* p. 182f.

15. *Jesus-God and Man,* tr. L. L. Wilkins and D. A. Priebe (London, 1968) p. 350.

16. 'Current Problems in Christology', *Theological Investigations* I, tr. C. Ernst (London, 1961) pp. 158ff.

17. Quoted by H. G. Gadamer, *Truth and Method,* tr. G. Barden and J. Cumming (London, 1975) pp. 179, 181.

18. *The Crucified God,* p. 6.

19. 'King Alfred's *aestel', Anglo-Saxon England,* ed. P. P. Clemoes 3 (Cambridge, 1974) pp. 109–110.

20. *The Cross in English Life and Devotion* (London, 1972) p. 14.

21. My *The Calvary Christ* (London, 1977) discusses the theme of 'Christ the Champion' at greater length; see pp. 3ff.

22. *A Marxist Looks at Jesus* (London, 1976) p. 154. This book is the finest book on Jesus so far produced by an atheist Marxist.

23. 'The Apocalyptic Myth and the Death of Christ', *Bulletin of the John Rylands University Library of Manchester* 57 (1975) p. 384.

NOTES to G. O'Collins, 'Reflecting Further':

1. *Models of the Church* (New York, 1974).

2. *The Church in the Power of the Spirit,* tr. M. Kohl (London, 1977) pp. 85–86.